COOL STU

I've made the biggest TV shows in the world with the biggest audiences, teams, budgets and stars, so I know the harsh reality of brutal feedback. One slip and you're on the news, front page of the papers and trending globally on Twitter. I've been there – more times than I can remember. Luckily, I found the bad stuff funny. If I hadn't, it would've killed me.

Flawsome arms you with tools and insights to be kind to and care for the most important person in your life – you.

It's like holding a big mirror up to your face, so close it mists up. It makes you want to look deeply at yourself and into yourself and do so with a kindness, honesty and wisdom that lacks judgement and celebrates your best you.

There is both wisdom and kindness in the pages, but also such tough love and raw honesty, that it's obvious Georgia lives what she writes.

Give this book to every 20-year-old you know so they can enjoy the wisdom that comes with being 50 right now, before they start to make a noise when getting out of low chairs.

– **Maz Farrelly**, Former TV producer; current speaker, trainer and media and communications specialist

From Australia's leading thinker, author and expert on feedback comes a new book on the most important feedback of all… the feedback we give ourselves. *Flawsome* is a book about our self-talk, and yet it's much more than that. It's a blueprint for how to be the best leader you can be, by doing the work on yourself to be the best person you can be. It's a book about acceptance and surrender; about forgiveness and responsibility; about evolving – not through fixing what's wrong but being okay with what is. It's a beautiful book, written with courage, humour and love. It's a leadership book, a personal development book and a spiritual book written with a deep wisdom that's been hard earned. Read this if you want to be a better leader or a better person, or just be a bit more comfortable in your skin. I loved it, and think you will too.

– **Peter Cook**, Chairperson, Thought Leaders Global

This book is an eye-opener and a heart-opener. I can't resist saying it: *Flawsome* is awesome! Georgia Murch takes us on an extraordinary journey right into the underbelly of our hearts and minds, with care and her beautifully honest style. She helps us examine our shadows, faults and internal wobbles with compassion and insight. There is so much to love about this book, including Georgia sharing the lived experience of embracing her own flawsomeness. It gave me the courage to examine some sticky bits in myself and 'eat some old beliefs' that were no longer serving me. If you're up for a real, up close, and sometimes uncomfortable examination of your flaws and ready to step into them as friends and teachers, get turning these pages!

– **Tracey Ezard**, Author of *The Buzz* and *Glue*, expert in education and learning and keynote speaker

In a culture where surface is valued more than substance (like most cosmetic surgery), where 'perfectionistic programming' is everywhere (think Instagram influencers, advertising et al.), where truth is being attacked daily (the fake news phenomenon), there emerges a clear, courageous voice of compassion, wisdom and honesty. We are all flawed. And therein lies our uniqueness, our strength, our purpose. Being flawsome is the challenge of this book. Read it.

– **Colin James**, Top-ranking global speaker, facilitator, educator and founder of the Colin James Method

Flawsome is the release valve leaders, parents and evolutionaries need to let go of the pressure we place on ourselves to be perfect. With personal candour and her trademark humour, Georgia Murch takes us on an exploration of what it truly takes to learn and grow in today's high-performance world. She encourages us to embrace our flawsomeness, by learning to process the feedback around us in ways that help us move from self-control to self-evolve. Packed full of tools for self-examination, tips for boosting relationships and laugh-out-loud stories about life and leadership, this book is for anyone ready to take their flaws and turn them into flawsome!

– **Dr Kelly Windle**, Vice-President Organisation Capability, BlueScope

What a thought-provoking tale of discovery and acceptance of humanities *Flawsome* is! As individuals, we have a unique ability to choose – to step into the good, to refute the bad and to embrace our own truth. On this journey, Georgia offers the opportunity of self-reflection, awareness and support through her own vulnerability.

– **Erin Clarke**, Human Resource Director A&NZ, Moët Hennessy

Georgia has written a must-read for anyone who has the courage to be flawsome! It's such a powerful message to own your flaws, embrace them, be curious. After all, it's the flaws that make you who you are. *Flawsome* is a great reminder that we all get to decide the story, we are the authors of our journey.

– **Michelle Ridsdale**, Chief People Officer, Envato

Georgia has done it again! The Queen of Feedback has perfectly distilled the art of communicating with, understanding and accepting oneself. It's only from this position that we can thrive. Whenever I spend time with Georgia, or read one of her books, I leave with a feeling of growth, curiosity, love, understanding and discomfort (some might call them growing pains). Do yourself a favour, pick up this book and start your journey to knowing your flawsome self, you won't regret it!

– **Matthew Bromley**, Managing Director, South East Asia, Haworth

FLAWSOME

THE JOURNEY TO BEING WHOLE IS LEARNING TO BE HOLEY

GEORGIA MURCH

I hope you find your flawsome G :)

First published in 2020 by Major Street Publishing Pty Ltd
E | info@majorstreet.com.au
W | majorstreet.com.au
M | +61 421 707 983

 A catalogue record for this
book is available from the
National Library of Australia

ISBN: 978-0-6487963-0-5

Cover design by Tess McCabe
Cover photographs by Rachel Callender
Internal design by Production Works
Printed in Australia by Ovato, an Accredited ISO AS/NZS 14001:2004 Environmental Management System Printer.

10 9 8 7 6 5 4 3 2 1

CONTENTS

FOREWORD

Before committing to anything of consequence, I like to ask three quick questions:

1. Can I back it up?

2. Is it important, worthwhile or valuable?

3. Is it coming from a good place, such as decency, humility, love or care?

I say this as a warning, because in your hand is the work of someone who has answered yes to all three: Georgia Murch.

As a consequence, I ask: 'Are you prepared to have your mind changed?' If you are – and this is your motivation for picking up this book – by turning its pages, you will be compelled to act.

Go deep to go forward.

Georgia's power is in her authenticity, a combination of generosity, kindness and sometimes disconcerting 'straightforwardness'. She knows that to be these things, you must be prepared to be vulnerable... to be flawsome.

Georgia models the T.D. Jakes leadership trust mantra: 'Our words tell others what we think. Our actions tell them what we believe'. Her book makes being flawsome possible, and after I read it, I thought she has actually defined the 'strategic advantages' of flawsomeness:

- **It's easier.** You don't have to make up who you are each time you walk in the room. You can be you.

- **It's real.** Stuff happens in your life over which you have no control whatsoever. That's okay. We understand.

- **It's powerful.** By showing your flawsomeness, you are drawing people closer to you, as well as creating space; it's an invitation for somebody to help you.

To make change happen, you are in charge, and in your hand is a way forward.

Flawsome will find you wherever you are now, with your current sense of self and understanding and it will help you to take on the world. It won't leave you where it found you. You will be changed, different in the important small ways.

This book is a gift. Georgia's gift. It is now your gift.

Cameron Schwab – Longest-serving CEO of three Australian Football League clubs; current author, facilitator, keynote speaker, expert in high performance and an all-round great human

ACKNOWLEDGEMENTS

They say it takes a village to raise a child. Well, it takes a tribe to be able to do life with energy and resolve, and my tribe is the best there is. Just sayin'.

Annie and James, you provided the place for me, and for many, to start reconciling this whole flawsome journey. To learn that who we are, as we are, is enough. You pioneered something new in a community that was stuck in old ways. So much love and respect to you both.

Peter Cook, you are a General, a five-star, a great friend and divine mentor. Your ability to teach much with few words is remarkable – something we could all aspire to. My practice and my character are better because of you.

Lesley Williams, my publisher, it's been smooth sailing from the beginning. What an easy ride to go on. Thank you. And Brooke Lyons, my editor, thanks for 'getting me' from the beginning and letting my voice shine through.

To the tribe I do life with, you know who you are. I would not be me without you. You have accepted me as I am. You have consistently given me permission to be flawsome and shown me I am awesome regardless. You don't let me hide. You never let me fall. You are the best group of humans a gal could ever know. If we were an army we would never be defeated.

To those who might not feel I'm their cup of tea, thank you. Thank you for allowing me to see my triggers. My learnings here have often been my greatest.

To my kids, Holly and Jacko (if you ever read this), you have both taught me so much. You have allowed me to see my whole self through parenting. As you grow older the roles are reversed and I am now learning from you (and loving it). I am excited to grow with you and grateful you've chosen to stay so close to your dear ol' ma.

THE INTRO BIT

I've spent the last ten years becoming known as the expert in designing feedback cultures in teams and organisations. It's been a passion project from the beginning, mainly born from a place of wanting the best conditions possible for people to thrive at work and home. But what I've increasingly seen and experienced, and in my own evolution, is that the feedback we give *ourselves* has a direct impact on how we speak and 'be' – with ourselves as well as those around us.

THE FEEDBACK WE GIVE *OURSELVES* HAS A DIRECT IMPACT ON HOW WE SPEAK AND 'BE' – WITH OURSELVES AS WELL AS THOSE AROUND US.

The pursuit of being truly human is discombobulating. We are so damn tough on ourselves. Whether we're aware of it or not, we end up projecting how we feel about ourselves on to others. Our expectations of others rise and fall based on what we expect from ourselves.

My initial hypothesis was that in order to make peace with our humanity we needed to drop our search for perfection.

We needed to be okay with being *enough* – flaws and all, no need for comparisons. At times I've been able to achieve this, so I know it's a fabulous place to be, and I wanted to help others get to the same place. What I didn't realise is that achieving peace is actually far easier than we all think. The answer, I believe, is: being flawsome.

FLAWSOME IS NOT JUST MAKING PEACE WITH YOUR FLAWS; IT'S KNOWING THAT WITHOUT THEM, YOU WOULD NOT BE YOU.

Flawsome is being who you are. It goes beyond making peace with your flaws; it means owning them, understanding them and knowing that admitting them gives you power – it doesn't take your power away. Flawsome can be raw, hard, exposing, realigning, reimagining (even when you feel like you are all out of imagination); it can undo you. But the work to embrace flawsome is absolutely worth it.

I thought the answer to inner peace would involve the feedback we give ourselves: what that is, how it needs to be rewired, what to believe and what *not* to. But it's so much more. It's deeper. It has a ripple effect beyond measure and a timing without boundaries.

To be flawsome involves not just accepting your flaws, your inadequacies and the things you hide; it's understanding where they come from, and rewriting how you see yourself, so you can live as you are. It's not just making peace with your flaws; it's knowing that without them, you would not be you. That's right: your flaws make you, you. They make you awesome, if you make peace with them and learn from them.

This book is for those who feel they need to use their abilities to be 'enough' for others; that serving others makes them whole. (Being generous is a beautiful thing, but there's a better way.) It's for those who are capable in their field, but still have a voice in their head that says, 'Someone will find me out'. It's for those who are aware of their flaws and think they need to wrestle them down.

I assumed that as soon as we recognised and rewrote the stories of our past we would be able to lead a flawsome life; that nature and nurture made us who we are. What I now know is that real freedom of heart, mind and soul comes from living in alignment with who we are called to be.

You are not called to be an accountant, a speaker or a cabinet maker. You are called by a name – *your* name. You are called to be *you*. But to know what that means and who *you* are requires work. Just like growing into a new pair of sneakers, you need to grow into who you really are.

Life and experiences get in the way and tell us something different. Life tells us we need to win to be a winner; that no-one will look out for us, so we need to become self-reliant. Life tells us we need to get great marks to have a great career, and that a great career alone will make us happy.

And you know what? We all believed it to be true.

This book will help you rewrite those truths. Let's stop relying on beliefs that don't serve us. Let's not fake it till we make it. You can't be sustained on things that are not real, and not true.

People ask me all the time, 'Georgia, how do I *really* become a good leader/friend/parent/lover/human?'. The 'You already are' answer does not suffice here, and it's pretty unhelpful. So, my answer is, 'Do the work'. This book will show you how.

You might be wondering who I am to be suggesting a path that could help you find your inner flawsome. I mean, you might be thinking WTF girl – you are an accountant by trade, a corporate refugee, and a speaker, trainer and author by choice. You didn't study psychology; you didn't write a thesis. If you're thinking all this, you're right. But, in the words of Malcolm Gladwell, I've done my 10,000 hours and then some. I have had so many conversations with people about how to talk to themselves and others that I'm sitting at well over 10,000 hours.

The thing is:

- I'm not a psychologist, but I study psychology.

- I'm not a counsellor, but I counsel.

- I'm not a doctor, but I do love to help others heal.

I interviewed hundreds of people in the process of putting this book together; I've worked with and listened to more than 20,000 people in my career, across all races, religions and personality types. I love people, I am fascinated by our humanity and if my work helps one person and that one person helps another and so on, then it counts!

Your challenge is to find the gold – for you. Seek out the content in this book that truly resonates and take it as far as you like.

And then, of course, I'll welcome all the feedback. Especially the stuff that comes with love. ;-)

PART I

THE PURSUIT OF FLAWSOME

1

LEARNING TO BE HOLEY

I first came across the phrase 'flawsome' years ago when I heard it coined by Tyra Banks. Tyra is a supermodel and the creator and executive producer of *America's Next Top Model*. She is one of the pioneering African American supermodels following in the footsteps of Naomi Campbell in what was once a white-dominated industry. She became the first ever African American to be on the cover of the Victoria's Secret catalogue, and was a catwalk model with them until 2005. She has pushed against racism for her entire career, but that isn't all she has stood against.

During her career Tyra was dropped from modelling and designer contracts after she put on some weight, because she was considered to be too curvy. Rather than starving herself and conforming to the industry standards, she decided to embrace her look and work with agencies who chose to do the same.

Tyra stands for being flawsome. She chooses to celebrate her 'flaws' and see them as what make her awesome; to rejoice in her humanity and not hide from it. She decided that her aim wasn't perfection, it was distinction. How cool is that?

Not long after Tyra started producing *America's Next Top Model*, photos appeared in the tabloids showing her in a swimsuit with noticeable curves and cellulite. The photos were featured alongside an article titled: 'America's Next Top Waddle'. She was working in an industry that expected and aimed for perfection, but this only spurred her on more. As a judge on the TV show, she taught women and men to highlight the things about themselves that were different from the 'norm': highlight your freckles, celebrate your curves, love your nose that's bigger or teeth that have gaps between them. Make your flaws your own.

Tyra is committed to using her platform to help everyone, especially young women, embrace their imperfections such as weight fluctuations, weird facial features and crooked teeth. I know, it's easy for her to do this when she looks like an Amazonian goddess. But the point is, celebrating your flawsomeness in an industry that doesn't rate imperfections is *big*. She has taken a stand against body shaming.

Tyra Banks and her flawsomeness got me thinking. If her legacy is about celebrating physicality in all its forms, why can't we do the same for our humanity? Why can't we choose to see the things about ourselves that we've decided are not cool as a unique part of us – part of what makes us human and perfectly flawed?

Tyra taught me that being flawsome means accepting *all* of yourself. This doesn't mean you love all of yourself all of the time; being flawsome requires you to constantly reframe your thoughts, especially if, like me, you are starting to nudge your 50s and bits are sagging that you never knew you had. But I am committed to my own evolution, and I am getting stronger at observing my judgement rather than latching on to it.

To be flawsome is to know that the things we think, what we look like, how we perform and how we fail are part of who we are. Instead of hiding from our flaws, we own them. We wear them with less judgement and more understanding. We make friends with the parts of ourselves that we have typically judged as flaws; as holes in our self; as bits that are missing or not right.

The journey to being whole is learning to be holey. To sit with who we are; to celebrate ourselves in all our holey-ness.

HONOURING YOUR CRACKS

Japan is an amazing country that I travelled to with my kids and good friends, the Laytons, in the Christmas of 2018. I was blown away by the kindness of the people, the incredible countryside and the orderly and respectful way that millions and millions of people, who live pretty much on top of each other, make it work. The Japanese appreciate their culture and are very pragmatic about how they live. It's amazing what they can fit into small places and how resourceful they are. There are no bins on the streets, which forces people to take their rubbish with them – to a home the size of a shoebox (well, compared to an Australian home, anyway). Recycling is second nature for them; excessive consumption is not.

The Japanese have a practice known as *Kintsukuroi,* which literally means 'gold mending'. It's a process that repairs broken objects, like cups and bowls, with gold. Instead of throwing objects away, they are beautified. According to art historians, the practice came about in the 15th century when a *shogun* (military leader) named Ashikaga Yoshimasa sent his favourite tea bowl to China to be repaired and it came back stapled together. It was so poorly done that his local craftsmen were asked to repair it with a gold lacquer. They did a much better job, and the bowl looked unique and became more valuable. The repair turned a problem into a plus. The art of *honouring* broken things and highlighting the breaks, instead of *hiding* them, became a thing.

Imagine if we knew that when something about us was broken, or we discovered a crack (as we all do), that we would be given gold. Wouldn't we just want to find more flaws? You'd have people lining up to declare their brokenness, right? (Okay, maybe that's too far, but you get my point.)

HIDING OUR FLAWS DOES NOT SERVE US; NOR DOES IT CELEBRATE WHO WE REALLY ARE.

If we didn't have these cracks, maybe we wouldn't be as valuable. To celebrate this is to honour ourselves and our humanity. Hiding our flaws does not serve us; nor does it celebrate who we really are.

2

YOUR FLAWSOMENESS
DRAWS PEOPLE TO YOU

Now, we've established that being flawsome is about embracing your flaws and celebrating your humanness. Have you ever heard a religious or spiritual leader, or any other person the world values, say you need to go and work on being perfect? So why do we feel the constant need to pursue perfection in mind, body and soul?

Aiming for peace with who you are can also be hard work; and it's much more rewarding, and requires less effort, less striving and less self-punishment than the impossible pursuit of perfection.

I've been following Celeste Barber on Instagram for a while now. She's become a global icon. Celeste made a name for herself via her #celestechallengeaccepted social media series, which began in 2015 as 'a fun experiment to see what it would look like for an average person to photograph herself doing rich-people things'. Celeste's re-enactments of celebrity and model photos complete with weird poses and outfits are LOL-worthy; she takes the mickey out of these people and exaggerates her own flaws for humour. My favourite re-enactment was one she did of Gwyneth Paltrow. In Gwyneth's shot we see her lying on her back, half naked, looking super-sexy and covered in a smooth, light brown mud with her hair back and a 'natural' face of make-up. She looks radiant. Celeste's version features the comedian lying in the same pose with half-dried, black lumpy mud on her body, curves and bumps on show, complete with a moustache of black mud.

I think the reason we love Celeste so much (aside from the LOLs she inspires) is that she is real. She is not hiding her body; she is saying, 'This is me, I am flawsome'. And she's made a living from it. With 9 million social media followers and counting, a flourishing comedy career and a book deal, she is doing just fine. Because of her strong following she was able to raise a staggering $51 million for the Australian bushfire appeal. People know she's authentic; we tend to trust others who are real. There is no pretence about who Celeste Barber is, or what she stands for.

WE ARE DRAWN TO PEOPLE NOT FOR THEIR PERFECTION, BUT FOR THEIR ACCEPTANCE OF THEIR IMPERFECTIONS.

Think about it: we are drawn to people not for their perfection, but for their acceptance of their imperfections. We might admire people who seem flawless, but they are hard to connect with and understand, and very hard to be like. It's our pursuit of perfection that's the problem.

I used to avoid putting up videos of myself on social media. If we did decide to do a video – for example, to promote an event – I would leave it till the absolute last minute because I felt so uncomfortable. Eventually I would shoot the video, then have to redo it, then redo it again: the words weren't right, the angle was wrong, the tone wasn't exactly as it was supposed to be. It held us back. The market wanted to see short, quick sound bites yet I was sticking to written blogs and newsletters because I wasn't perfect in videos. I made my perfection a greater priority than getting messages that could help others out to the market.

Then my good friend, author and marketing strategist Brent Hodgson, introduced me to the concept of the 'Pratfall Effect'. A pratfall is a stupid or humiliating action – like when you fall on your backside in the middle of the street in front of everyone or get tongue tied when you are speaking (or forget what you were saying altogether). What happens when we do this, as long as it's not all the time, is that our appeal to others *increases*. Yep, you're actually considered *more likeable* when you make a blunder, as long as you have shown your credibility first.

Elliot Aronson first described the Pratfall Effect in 1966 and lots of studies have been done since to prove the theory. One study looked at the likeability and trust we have in doctors of psychiatry, comparing those who spilt their coffee or dropped their pen (a physical pratfall) in their initial meeting with those who didn't. The results showed that people felt more drawn to those who made a mistake. The point is that, when others make mistakes, we feel more sympathetic towards them; we get to see their human side.

SHOWING YOUR VULNERABILITY INCREASES YOUR CONNECTION WITH OTHERS.

The Pratfall Effect says that if you want to build trust quickly with people, showing your flaws is one way to do this. Showing your vulnerability *increases your connection* with others. This seemed like a Willy Wonka Golden Ticket to me. You mean I can cough, or fall over my words, or even forget what I am saying for a second? WTF? That is revolutionary. It meant that I had permission to be me – think light bulbs and fireworks. These days, I mostly do my videos in one take. I don't care if I make mistakes. It makes me flawsome!

The bottom line is that we don't easily trust people who seem too perfect, yet we live in a paradox where perfect is seen as better and anything less is failure. This is a trap. The pursuit of perfection is holding us back from connecting with others and ourselves – because we stay in judgement, not observation. And that can be an exhausting place to live in.

3

AN UNHEALTHY RELATIONSHIP
WITH FEEDBACK

If you opened your email right now and saw a message with the subject, 'I want to make a time to give you some feedback', what would you think? Honestly, what's your first gut reaction? If you're like most people, you will assume the worst. We are all a little cray cray like that.

INNER PEACE IS DIFFICULT TO ACHIEVE WHEN WE ARE CONSTANTLY ANTICIPATING THE WORST.

We are wired to think in deficits. The technical term is a 'negative bias'. Simply put, our brains have a greater sensitivity to negative news – to the point where we anticipate it. When we see good stuff, like videos of cute cats and incredible landscapes, we have a surge of stimuli in our brain. When we see pictures of starving children or hurt animals, there is an even greater surge of activity. We are wired like this to protect ourselves from danger – even if the danger is to our happiness. Our brains are trying to keep us out of harm's way. But inner peace is difficult to achieve when we are constantly anticipating the worst – especially if our worries are playing in our heads at an unhelpful volume.

This psychological phenomenon is why we tend to dwell on criticism or bad news: our brain responds to it at a greater level. It's why bad first impressions can be so hard to move on from, and past traumatic events have such a lingering effect. Negativity stimulates us so much we remember the feeling and don't want to experience it again, so we are 'on alert' most of the time.

Think about this. You are on a train and you hear a group of people talking about how lovely one of their co-workers is. Then you hear a different group of people complaining about a bully at work. Which conversation will you be most drawn to? The data tells us we will be far more drawn to the discussion about the bully, because our brain will have reacted more strongly to it. The same goes for what you focus on. Think about a few examples of when someone has told you something negative. It could be something about the meal you cooked or bought, how you laughed too loudly, some negative feedback about your work or someone telling you that you're coming across as uncaring. Next, try to think of some examples of when someone appreciated who you are or what you did.

Now ask yourself – which examples were easier to recall? Which are you ruminating on – the positive comments or the ones that highlighted a deficit?

Our brains are wired to stay in the trap of anticipating bad news; but it doesn't have to be that way. In fact, thinking this way will not serve you, because you will assume the worst and then go down a rabbit warren of being constantly on your guard and defensive, or even retreating.

The thing about feedback is that it's not always about what people tell us. It's not always the content in conversations. Feedback is everywhere and can be conveyed in a multitude of ways. It could be a casual conversation with someone, or observing how someone is treating another person. If someone is yelling at a child and you have a reaction to it (in this case, it's likely to be unease), that's feedback you are receiving that you are uncomfortable.

Feedback could be a silent look in your direction in a meeting or at a cafe. You might think 'the look' means the person is interested in chatting, or it might mean they want you to talk more quietly – it could even be that they are just scanning the room. Whatever you make that look mean – is feedback.

Let's say you're waiting for the train and discover it will be five minutes late. You're annoyed; that's feedback. You read an article on Facebook about climate change and can feel your pulse rate rising. That's also feedback.

We need to be conscious of how our brain works to decipher what is valuable to process and take on board from the feedback we receive, and what is not. This will allow us to be open and not on edge. When we make peace with our flawsomeness, feedback will just become news: information that we can decide to learn from, or put to the side. To know that we don't have to agree or disagree with information that comes towards us, and that we can choose whether or not to receive feedback, is the key.

Seth Godin, multiple bestselling author and 'ultimate entrepreneur', is always a great source of pearls of wisdom. He says: 'One piece of feedback is not the source of truth'. He says we can skew our thinking based on the first piece of feedback we receive: 'That's the moment of maximum fragility, and so our radar is on high alert'. In other words, our stress radar is in action mode, so we might grip on to feedback – particularly feedback we receive early in a project or relationship – as if it's the truth. But remember: feedback is just one perspective; it may be useful, or it may not. You get to decide.

Feedback is just information you receive, and how you respond to it. Both the receiving and responding are feedback: one is feedback that comes your way, and the other is feedback you give yourself.

FEEDBACK IS INFORMATION WE CAN CHOOSE TO TAKE ON BOARD AND LEARN FROM, OR DISCARD.

Feedback is information we can choose to take on board and learn from, or discard. It will always have the power to make us bitter or make us better. Motivational speaker Jay Shetty says, 'Bitterness broods and better grows'. I think he's 100 per cent right. There is nothing to be gained from becoming frustrated at someone or the feedback they have given us; that eats us alive. Choosing to grow from the experience is a happier place and one that serves us. The cool news is that we hold that power; we just need to learn how to use the power well. It's kinda like becoming a feedback Jedi.

4
IT STARTS WITH *YOU*

My good friend Lucas (one of my favourite humans) always says that you can't solve an internal problem with an external solution. I just love that. Lucas is super-experienced in this space; he spent 15 years as an addict. He tried everything under the sun to not only numb his emotional state but to try to find his happy. He and his wife Erin have now radically turned their lives around from addiction and destruction to serving the world around them in a super-significant way. I have so much respect for them. He is nine years sober now, and one of the coolest guys I know.

Lucas often says that addiction is when your solution becomes your problem. It's not always about drugs and alcohol; for many of us, it could be an unhealthy obsession with pleasing others, staying in a destructive relationship or the pursuit of physical perfection.

We need to be careful that our medication doesn't become our disease. We need to be conscious that we are not ignoring things in our life by replacing them with distractions that become a new pain for us to work through or shed.

If you are uncomfortable with your own thoughts and feelings, do you spend time on social media to distract yourself? All the data is proving that anxiety and depression increases when we compulsively use social media. Or do you self-medicate by being super-busy? If so, you are probably exhausted because you are doing too much. When we self-medicate, we often find ourselves with a new problem to solve – and the old one hasn't gone away either.

WE NEED TO BE CAREFUL THAT OUR MEDICATION DOESN'T BECOME OUR DISEASE.

You can't fail at one relationship and move to another thinking it will automatically be better. We throw food out when it is past its use-by date; why don't we do the same for our unhealthy thinking patterns and behaviours that don't serve us?

Making peace with who you are – with all your lumps and bumps, highs and lows and strengths and weaknesses – is being flawsome. Hiding from these things by replacing them with unhealthy habits only slows you down, and ultimately your quest for joy and happiness will fail.

It's not about high performance. Flawsome is about high acceptance, irrespective of whether you meet a goal or not.

We also can't expect the world, and all the people in it, to bend to our way of doing life, or to work around us so we can get what we need. Not only is this an impossible expectation, but at its core it is very self-focused; it is saying that my way is *the* way and you all need to change for me.

I get it though. If only others spoke less so we could get a word in. Or maybe they could contribute more and do their bit. If only they could speak with kindness or be less emotional. Whatever it may be that you need others to do more or less of, expecting this is still a form of control. You're saying, 'When you change, I can be more or better and life will be easier'. But the other person must do all the work; it's a transfer of responsibility and a form of blame. Ouch, right?

We can't expect others to change for us to be at peace. You can't make others see you as important. You can't do someone else's learning for them. This is not your role.

To achieve inner peace, we think we need our colleagues, our friends or our family to act differently, to speak differently, to just *be* different. That's like asking someone else to go to the hairdresser for you. Yeah, nah. *We* have to do the work. We must work to understand what's going on, our reaction to it, how we can learn from it and then rewire to be better. It starts with how we respond in situations with people we love, and those we struggle to love. We can learn from people we know deeply and even those we've just met or even never will. Every person and circumstance provides an opportunity to learn and grow, yet we push these learning opportunities away.

IT'S NOT ABOUT HIGH PERFORMANCE. FLAWSOME IS ABOUT HIGH ACCEPTANCE, IRRESPECTIVE OF WHETHER YOU MEET A GOAL OR NOT.

We can learn about ourselves through our everyday interactions. Did you judge the Uber driver when you hopped in the car, or before they were even there? Did you find yourself being short? Did you treat them as a human, or a service? Every interaction is an opportunity to learn.

What about how you are with your family? Now that's a trigger for many and sometimes it feels like there is no learning to be had. But these interactions can be unopened gifts; a bit like gold. Gold is hard to find – you have to search for special places in the earth and the sea to source it. But when you do find it, it's very valuable. Finding the gift in your experiences with others can feel like that too. The gold is hard to find, but super-valuable when you do.

5

FINDING YOUR EVOLUTION

If we want to start understanding ourselves, part of the journey is learning about how we connect and react to things around us. If we ignore this, we are just an island. An island cannot self-sustain long-term; it eventually needs other resources and the land to be tended for it to continue to survive. We need other people, who become our fuel, to live well.

The ultimate flawsome state is one where we never stop learning and growing and we accept that this is the best way to be. It means we are in a permanent state of evolution. Evolution doesn't have an end date; it keeps going to infinity. Any information that comes our way — whether it's what we tell ourselves or what we learn from others — is just that: information. It's something to understand, look at and learn from.

**THE ULTIMATE FLAWSOME STATE IS
ONE WHERE WE NEVER STOP LEARNING
AND GROWING.**

There may be some spaces in your life where you feel you are in a permanent state of growth and you are aware of what is happening and able to suspend judgement – of others and yourself. But most of us are always wavering in our learning. Some days are great, some are not. In some moments we excel, and others we react poorly. That's okay. The journey to flawsome is not linear; it ebbs and flows. It's your intent that's important.

Let's look at some of the phases we can move in and out of to grow into a state of evolution.

OUR INTENT	OUR STATE	OUR GROWTH		
With awareness	Comes evolution	∞	From a place of surrender	Above the line
With forgiveness	Comes acceptance	+100		
With ownership	Comes regulation	+10	From a place of responsibility	
With denial	Comes disconnection	-50	From a place of domination	Below the line
With blame	Comes assassination	-100		

You will see that there are 'above the line' and 'below the line' growth patterns. You may have heard about this as an accounting concept used to track revenue and expenses; in marketing, it is also used as a market segmentation tool. In our case, it's about ourselves.

Being above the line is about staying open and curious; responding well because your intention comes from a good place. Below the line is when you are closed, defending or protecting

– defending yourself either passively or explicitly and denying you have a role to play. It's about avoidance of responsibility.

The Conscious Leadership Group suggests we locate ourselves above or below the line because this 'helps us identify how we are being with what is occurring in our life right now'. Our behaviours have a direct correlation with what is going on for us inside, so this is an incredibly useful tool.

When you are not in growth you are likely to have a strong relationship with control, which is about dominating others and your thinking (being your own God). You decide who is right and wrong, and blame others for your situation – coming from a place of domination. This is a below-the-line state. Domination can look like trying to control your environment, your workplace rules and the people around you. It's when we need the people and things around us to change for us to be okay, or when we deny what is really going on. If you find yourself not wanting to accept the circumstances you find yourself in, or pretending things are not happening, you're probably in a below-the-line state.

When you start noticing how you are responding to the outside world and decide to respond well, you move into responsibility. This is where you manage your responses, understanding that there is a better way and that you must self-regulate.

WHEN YOU START NOTICING HOW YOU ARE RESPONDING TO THE OUTSIDE WORLD AND DECIDE TO RESPOND WELL, YOU MOVE INTO RESPONSIBILITY.

The opposite of domination is surrender. To surrender is to observe how people are behaving and what is happening in our world, but to know what we can influence and what we can leave. Surrender is a place where we know the only person we can control is ourselves, and therefore it comes from a place of love and self-acceptance.

All of these phases that we move in and through come from an intent. We may be conscious of our intent or not, but either way it has an impact – it influences how we are with others and with ourselves.

So, let's understand each phase and see if we can self-assess where we tend to land. Once you know that, you can work out what you need to do to reach your ultimate flawsome state. (Keep in mind, though, that we can move states within years or even minutes. It is not binary; it's evolutionary.)

We will start at the bottom of the ladder, to learn about our unhelpful behaviours and what causes them.

BLAME BREEDS ASSASSINATION

I've been practising yoga for more than 15 years now. I started not long after having my second child, Holly. I've learnt a lot about myself in yoga. At the start I would get so annoyed and frustrated: at myself for not getting into a pose or being able to hold it; at the heat (keep in mind I chose to go to Bikram yoga, which is 40 degrees and 40 poses); and at the teachers for not being clear enough, strong enough or kind enough.

I remember this one teacher; we will call her Tina. Tina was a strong woman – physically and, I presumed, psychologically. She was 6 foot tall with the physicality of a Serena Williams – and, it would seem, the same determination. When I registered at reception she would always give me a purposeful eyeball, say my name in a loud southern American accent and find a reason to give off a super-loud laugh that reverberated around the room.

Now, at 6 am, I was never feeling like a belly laugh. Starting the motor to get there in the first place was loud enough for me.

I did a lot of Tina's classes and over time her style really started to grate on me. Her instructions were always very clear and precise. Her encouragement, when we got the pose correct, was generous. But when we didn't get the pose right or we needed a rest, it was 'accusation on'. If the class was struggling to keep the pace or strength *that she expected*, she would often stop the class and make a statement. Some examples: 'Am I teaching the elderly class today?', or 'Is that the best you've got?'. Sometimes she would just laugh out loud and ask people to guess why she was laughing.

Lots of people liked her classes. She was strong and taught a strong class. She cracked gags and would often share a little anecdote. I, however, decided her comments were passive aggressive and that she was trying to shame us into submission. I decided she was wrecking my practice. When I went to the class and she was at reception I would do an internal sigh and have to self-manage myself through the class. This went on for a couple of years.

Then one day, I started learning about projection. I learned that the things we react to in others are often a reflection of our own behaviours. Ouch! Many of these behaviours exist in the shadows; that is, they are not easy to see. We blame or punish others for the things we don't like in ourselves. It's quite sub-conscious too.

THE THINGS WE REACT TO IN OTHERS ARE OFTEN A REFLECTION OF OUR OWN BEHAVIOURS.

Austrian neurologist Sigmund Freud first spoke of projection, and then worked with psychiatrist Carl Jung to further develop the theory; together they explored what happens when your ego is not willing to see certain parts of yourself. These days, there are a lot of experts in this space. One of my favourites is Byron Katie. The work she does to help people unlock what's getting in the way of them being their best is not about shame or blame; nor proving who is right and who is wrong. She says, 'The power of the turnaround lies in the discovery that everything you think you see on the outside is really a projection of your own mind. Everything is a mirror image of your own thinking'.

This is pretty cool if you think about. If you start becoming aware of what you see in others as a projection of yourself, you hold the key to your own evolution; you have the power to see, or not to see.

So, if I applied the theory of projection to how I felt about Tina, what then? My first reaction was to think, 'OMG! I can't be passive aggressive, can I?'. But when I dug deeper, I realised that, yep, passive aggressive is my default when I don't like what other people are doing or saying. It was tough to realise.

We are often so busy pointing out the splinters in others' eyes that we can't see the log that's sitting in our own. Blame is the discharge of truth. We need to understand the role blame plays in our life. When we blame, we shut our mind off to possibility. Blame becomes an excuse to avoid seeing another's perspective. I'm not suggesting here that everyone is without faults; what I mean is, if you learn to stand in other people's shoes, rather than blaming them, you might begin to understand their perspective. It doesn't mean you have to agree with everything they say and think, but you will have empathy. It will be easier for yourself to learn, and for others to be with you.

Blame is binary thinking: yes or no, good or bad. Blaming others isn't helpful, but neither is self-blame. And we can all fall into this habit easily.

We 'should' all over ourselves

As part of the research for *Flawsome* I interviewed hundreds of people. The questions focused on what 'giving yourself permission to be human' means, and how much people give themselves. I also asked about people's self-talk and actions when they are in a good space, or not. The hypothesis that I had at the start was that people would tell me that their pursuit of perfection was getting in the way of them giving themselves permission to be 'enough'; that their flaws held them back. There were components of this, but it was not the resounding theme.

Most suggested that allowing yourself to be human is about permission to be messy, to fail and to show weakness; being okay with not meeting expectations – your own and others'; giving yourself a break; and not being emotional when you make mistakes.

A smaller proportion said it is being brave enough to be who you really are – your authentic self. To know that you are a work in progress and always will be; to be real with yourself and others and realise that we are multidimensional beings.

The really interesting bit is that over 70 per cent of people asked me whether they should answer my questions in a work or life context. Others self-selected to talk about themselves in a work context. I did not expect the research to go there, or for people to be so definitive about the difference. This was an interesting surprise. It showed me that people see themselves as playing a role in a work environment, whereas in their private lives they are more comfortable with being themselves.

Yet the person we take to work is also the person we take home. Think about yourself like an orange. Whether you put that orange on the boardroom table, at the local coffee shop or at home in the kitchen, it's still an orange; the inside stays the same. It's the same for ourselves.

THE PERSON WE TAKE TO WORK IS ALSO THE PERSON WE TAKE HOME.

The 70 per cent who questioned the context of my interviews believe they are not supported in a work environment to be who they truly are; to show their humanity. It's still about permission, right? Permission to be who you really are – the at-home version of yourself.

It got me thinking: what holds people back from giving themselves permission to be who they really are, especially at work? One of the big reasons, I believe, is that we 'should' all over ourselves. My interviewees made these sorts of comments:

'I should have seen that coming.'

'I should have known that was going to happen.'

'I should have worked harder or smarter.'

'I should have achieved more by now.'

'I should have been around more for the kids or my partner.'

'I should have reacted differently.'

'I should have said nothing; done nothing.'

Interestingly, the more experience people had, the louder the voice became: 'I'm such an idiot. I'm so stupid'. We are more experienced at self-punishing than self-approving. When we believe we *should have* known better, this is driven from a place of shame. It serves no-one, but it's a common space we play in.

Where in your world are you asking or expecting another person to change to make your world easier? Where are you blaming another or a circumstance for being wrong because you are right? Where is your thinking binary?

Or are you in self-blame, and 'shoulding' all over yourself? When do you tell yourself you should have known better, should have done better or should be better? Assassination of others and of self becomes the result. Blame breeds assassination.

DENIAL BREEDS DISCONNECTION

Here's the funny thing about denial: you might not admit you are in it, or even be able to name it, but deep down something won't feel right. I love how my friend James Layton talks about denial: he says it's like walking around with a poo on your shoe thinking it is someone else's. How good is that?

Why do people stay in this place then? I can't presume to know anyone's exact reasons, but it will always come from a foundation of fear. Fear comes in many forms: fear of having to face up to parts of yourself that you do not like; fear of learning about those around you and the role you have let them play in your life; fear of having to take responsibility for the role you have played in your own life. Denial becomes a place where people can feel safe.

People in denial downplay the impact of other people or situations in their life. People who are highly defensive can be in denial that there is some truth in another's words. People who refuse to admit that they played a role in the failure of a relationship, a role or a decision are also in denial. (Stay with me. Don't go into denial now ;-))

The human brain is an incredible thing. It has the ability to reframe a situation, whether it serves us or not. This is called 'neuroplasticity'. The term was first used by Polish neuroscientist Jerzy Konorski in 1948 to describe how the neurons (cells) in our brain can change. The research morphed in the 1960s to show that our brain not only responds but can 'reorganise' itself, for good or bad. Like defragging a computer, our brain can do the same.

NO MATTER WHO YOU ARE, YOUR BRAIN HAS DEVELOPED COPING MECHANISMS TO HELP YOU DEAL WITH LIFE.

No matter who you are, your brain has developed coping mechanisms to help you deal with life. These coping mechanisms can be helpful or unhelpful. When our brains have an unhealthy response, it can become hard for us to address the real issues or make behavioural changes. It's basically a coping mechanism – we are blocking events or words from our conscious awareness. If there is something we don't want to address, or that feels too hard to cope with (especially when traumatic circumstances are involved), we simply refuse to accept it and sometimes even remember it. We pretend it's not real, and therefore doesn't have an impact on us.

It's like when your body goes into a coma to keep itself alive. Your mind does the same. It shuts out what it needs to in order to cope. Fear-based memories or experiences can sometimes lead to avoidance behaviours that can hold you back from living life to the fullest.

I have been told over the years, many times, that I can be intimidating. This feedback hasn't come from people of a particular gender, age or seniority – it seems it was people's experience of me, across the board. For years I honestly believed that people were just coming from a place of their own insecurity; that they needed to be stronger and 'less sensitive'.

In my heart I believed that you should be strong and speak your 'truth', and that other people should be open to hear it. This stance meant that it took me a long time to rewire my thinking. I was open to hearing other people's perspective of me, but I didn't believe what they were saying. On the other hand, if someone else intimidated me, did I believe they needed to soften or adapt their style? Abso-friggin-lutely. Oh, the irony.

The crunch came one year when I felt like I received a barrage of feedback about my style. I had taken on more responsibility and therefore accountability at work; and what I have learned over my career and after working with thousands of leaders is that the more you take on, the more people expect of you. That's just the way leadership works.

With my role growing, so too did others' expectations of me. Suddenly, the way I spoke to people and treated them was in the spotlight. I was told I could be short with people, and was sometimes dismissive. I was told I gave a particular 'look' when it appeared I didn't like what people were saying. I was also told that I cut people off and discounted their opinions.

Well, f*** me. The person they were describing was not the person I believed I was. But I also knew that awareness is a combination of what you believe *and* how others perceive you. BOOM! Hit the pain button. The pain of realising you are not the leader, or the person, you thought you were, that you've got work to do and that people avoid you, is tough to feel.

But I knew if I didn't feel it and take the feedback on board, I would stay in my bubble of denial. Staying in denial meant I could not grow.

I have stayed in denial in a few past relationships, too. I was in denial when a person I was with had very few close friends; I told myself that it was gorgeous that he wanted to be with me 24/7 because he loved me to bits. I ignored his jealousy and denied it would become a problem.

The thing about denial is that it is hard to see. You can see it in others, but it's much harder to spot in yourself. The good news is that we can all tap into our internal denial radar if we really try. Our bodies can detect when things aren't right, even when they appear so. Gut feel is a real thing. Have you ever noticed that feeling of nausea in your stomach when someone asks you to do something that is outside your comfort zone? Maybe you've noticed those butterflies in your tummy when you are about to meet someone who excites you; or the subtle and unexplainable feeling when something just isn't 'right'.

THE THING ABOUT DENIAL IS THAT IT IS HARD TO SEE. YOU CAN SEE IT IN OTHERS, BUT IT'S MUCH HARDER TO SPOT IN YOURSELF.

Those feelings that sometimes have no logical explanation are your 'gut feelings' or intuition. We're all familiar with the concept, but are we all on top of how to use it?

I'm a big believer in listening to my gut. I can recall when I first started exploring it; I was in my 20s, working in recruitment and would interview up to 15 people per week. My job was to make a call about which candidate was best suited to which client. The ultimate match was a combination of their skills and their cultural fit.

Some people looked amazing on paper, and in the interview they gave textbook-quality answers – but something told me I needed to be careful about them. At first, I had no idea why – until I placed them in a role and there were issues. What I learnt time and time again was that my gut feeling was a great gauge to help me understand who was a good fit, and who wasn't. My gut would tell me who I needed to interview more rigorously; I would ask those candidates more questions and do extra reference checks on them. My intuition became *another* tool that helped me be successful. If only I applied that to the dating decisions I've made in the past (insert eye roll); at 48 I am still learning.

We now know that our gut and our brain are connected, and the connection goes both ways. Our brain can affect our gut: a stressed or anxious brain can cause digestive and stomach issues. Think about those moments we spend on the toilet before having to do a presentation or ruminating over 'that' conversation. Our gut can also affect our brain. We all have neurotransmitters that go directly from our brain to our gut. The gut has even been described as our second brain.

Our brain recalls every decision, every meeting, every interaction, every conversation – whether it's conscious or unconscious. It stores a vast amount of information that we are not even aware of. It's like a jigsaw puzzle and the only pieces we have within our immediate reach are those we are conscious of.

It makes sense that as we gather more experiences in life, and understand and reflect on what our intuition told us in past situations, we are able to hone our intuition. If we make the space to reflect and learn, we can refine this tool. So when your intuition speaks – listen to it. Don't ignore it. Investigate it. Be aware of it.

I'm not saying you should make all your decisions based on gut feelings alone: if you don't have any facts or examples to prove your thinking, one way or the other, then be careful. But I am suggesting that your intuition is something that needs to be explored and understood.

Next time you suspect you might be living in denial, maybe you should start listening to your gut. What's wrong with being more open? You'll learn and others will find you easier to work with and be with. If you adamantly deny something – there might be something in it after all.

One thing to be mindful of is that delusion is different to denial. Delusion is where we actually believe our thinking about ourselves and others to be true, when it's not. When we are in a delusional state, we can't tell the difference between what's real and what's not. Karl Jaspers, psychiatrist and philosopher, suggested there are three criteria that need to be met for a belief to be diagnosed as delusional:

1. The false belief is held with absolute certainty or conviction.

2. The belief remains unchanged despite proof that it is not true.

3. The belief is false, implausible, bizarre or impossible.

If you believed that aliens implanted something in your mind, and you have memories of events that did not happen or even no acknowledgement of things that did, then it would seem like a delusional state. People in this state believe their thinking to be true. To an extent it would seem pointless asking yourself if you are delusional: how would you know? This is a dangerous place to be, and it's certainly dangerous to call people on it – so a bit of caution and compassion is needed here.

What we do know is that when we are in denial (or delusion for that matter), we create an obvious disconnection with ourselves. We don't face the truth, and our ability to build a deeper relationship with ourselves and others can flatline.

Are there any parts of your life that your gut tells you could be worthwhile exploring? Is there anything you are adamant about that others tell you that you could be incorrect about? Do you suspect there could be another way of thinking about something you feel strongly about? It's worth exploring. If you're not prepared to do the work to explore your potential areas of denial, you might be creating a disconnection with yourself and pushing away those around you. It might be lonely, and there's another way – a better way to live and be. Denial breeds disconnection.

OWNERSHIP BREEDS REGULATION

Taking responsibility for the impact you have requires a level of maturity and bravery. It's saying. 'I am aware of the role I play in others' lives and the impact I might have – on them and myself'. It's owning it; it's like putting your big boy, or girl, pants on.

These days, I own the fact that I could intimidate people. I take responsibility for when I am short with my kids, my work colleagues and people on the street. I know that I can shut down when I am with someone who presses my buttons, and that this might come across as disinterest. This doesn't mean I have transformed into love, light and happiness, but I am much more aware of my behaviour and how it affects others.

SOMETIMES IT'S REALLY HARD TO ACCEPT THE IMPACT WE HAVE ON THOSE AROUND US AND OURSELVES.

Sometimes it's really hard to accept the impact we have on those around us and ourselves. We become ashamed of our behaviour, and it feels painful. Sometimes we are willing to accept some things about ourselves, but others still stay on the shelf; that ol' denial popping its head up again. Regulating how you respond is self-control. That's a good thing; it's management of self. When you know how to do that, you make it easy for others to be around you. You also make yourself open to learning.

I know that when I am stressed, or put into situations I find taxing, I need to be careful not to lash out, or say something I regret. My natural response is to fight the situation or the person. I know I need to self-regulate during those times and not be passive aggressive (or even just plain aggressive). I realise I must stay open to the other person's perspective and be careful of my need to win or be right.

Others might fall into flight behaviours and just want to avoid the person, the conversation or the circumstance. If this is you, you have to own this and self-manage to stay in the conversation. Flighters might fall in the trap of passive agreement; that is, they say 'Yes, whatever you want' to avoid the conflict. Flighters need to be conscious of not shutting down or running away. Fighters need to replace being right with being curious. Flighters need to replace an exit strategy with an entry one.

Think about someone in your life, past or present, who always appears calm under pressure. When they get bad news or someone disagrees with them they remain in control. What we don't know is whether this is coming from a place of self-control, or if they are genuinely not affected by another's behaviour. By taking responsibility and self-managing, it is possible for us to remain still and controlled even in situations that disturb us.

FIGHTERS NEED TO REPLACE BEING RIGHT WITH BEING CURIOUS.

FLIGHTERS NEED TO REPLACE AN EXIT STRATEGY WITH AN ENTRY ONE.

The thing about responsibility is that it is freeing. It means we own our part. It means we are moving from being a toddler, who is unaware of how they connect with and impact others, to being a grown-up and taking responsibility for our actions by self-regulating.

This goes back to why we often say we are different at work than we are at home. Usually it's because we exercise more self-control at work because we don't feel as safe to be ourselves. Here's the thing: self-management all the time can be tiring, because it is coming from a place of management – it's not a natural response. Yet we know it's a mature one. Ownership breeds regulation.

Are there circumstances in your world where you know you self-manage rather than react naturally? Are there people who you know who require some deep breaths before you connect with them? The good news is that there is an easier place to operate from that will allow you to be with those people and ultimately with yourself. It's about forgiveness.

FORGIVENESS BREEDS ACCEPTANCE

I've been going to Narcotics Anonymous (NA) meetings to support one of my dear friends. She hit a milestone in her recovery, which was 90 days clean. It was incredibly special to be there and see her celebrated; she received her '90-day chip' for getting through one of the toughest experiences of her life.

For those of you who are not aware of what an NA meeting involves, in essence it creates a space where people can openly process where they are at. They are given the chance to share what's going on for them for up to five minutes, with no judgement and no advice. They can just be whatever they like and say whatever they want. And they do. If you are precious, then this is not a place for you. It's real and raw.

The theme for this particular meeting was the 12 Steps. The 12 Steps is a set of guiding principles providing a road map for recovery from addiction. Members of this particular meeting were asked to reflect on the impact of the 12 Steps on their recovery. I noticed that people kept referring to Step 4 – 'Made a searching and fearless moral inventory of ourselves' – as being one of the toughest to move through. This step is apparently the one that people can get consistently stuck on; at worst, it could throw people back to using again.

What is Step 4 really asking? It's about doing a deep and personal – and often confronting – inventory of who we really are, and our past and current behaviours. It means being ruthlessly honest about where we are at and have been. I can see why this caused some people to get stuck.

When we do things we are not proud of, make decisions that don't serve us or those around us, or dislike (or even hate and loathe) traits about ourselves, we often live in shame. The thing about shame is that it secretive. We hide these feelings and thoughts, and it can be extremely uncomfortable to wrestle with and understand them.

What the members of NA are learning, in the meetings and via Step 4, is to understand the antidote to shame: to shine a light on our darker thoughts and feelings that we are not proud of. When we acknowledge and start to understand our flaws, shame has nowhere to hide. Vulnerability is the antidote to shame. Brené Brown nails it in *Daring Greatly* when she says:

> *Vulnerability sounds like truth and feels like courage. Truth and courage aren't always comfortable, but they're never weakness. Because true belonging only happens when we present our authentic, imperfect selves to the world, our sense of belonging can never be greater than our level of self-acceptance.*

The thing about forgiveness is that it is not a gift for another person: It's your gift. It means you can move forward and release the angst and burden that you've been holding on to. Forgiveness of self is the harder one to do.

We love a bit of self-flagellation, don't we? (Hopefully nothing like Silas, the priest in *The Da Vinci Code*, who whips himself repeatedly. Whoa, that was next level.) Even if we don't physically harm ourselves, we can self-flagellate in our minds. We ruminate on our wrongs; most of us have an ever-present enemy that sits on our shoulders and whispers (or yells) in our ear. Guilt is the emotion that drives our need to beat up on ourselves for what we are ashamed of having done or are doing, or didn't do that we should have done. The more guilty we feel, the less able we are to forgive ourselves.

The perfectionists among us really have it bad. They are stricken with guilt because everything they do is not as perfect as it 'should' be. Then there are those of us who tend to worry about what others might think, even when we are doing what is right for ourselves. That's not so much a question of guilt as it is shame; it's a lack of feelings of worth.

Of course, guilt and shame are closely related. Guilt comes from our actions or behaviours, but if what we do makes us feel ashamed of who we are, then shame is added to the guilt. Shame is related to who we are as people: 'I did something wrong; therefore, I am a bad person'.

I connect with Colin Tipping in his book *Radical Self-Forgiveness* (which we will return to later):

> *Once we recognize that what we see and criticize in others is simply a reflection of what we can't stand in ourselves, it becomes clear that we are being given an opportunity to heal the split within ourselves. By taking back all our projections and loving the parts of us we had previously hated, we expand into love for ourselves and return ourselves to wholeness.*

Learning to be okay with where we are at and learning from our experiences is the next step. This is flawsome. And it requires forgiveness, including forgiveness of self – one of the hardest things to do.

Forgiveness facilitates a place where we stop needing to control ourselves and those around us, and practise the art of surrendering: surrendering to what's happened and accepting it. To get to a place of self-acceptance you need to start with loving yourself in all your flawsomeness. Forgiveness is the start. Forgiveness breeds acceptance.

AWARENESS BREEDS EVOLUTION

Awareness is an incredible state. It comes from a place where your eyes are wide open to the possibilities of self, others and new ideas. In a state of awareness, you can see how you react to yourself and others and learn from it. Getting into this state requires us to drop our aims and expectations.

Sometimes awareness comes easily because we are not attached to an outcome; we are open to what will be. Let's be real though: it might not always be effortless. Being open means accepting the pain and discomfort that comes with it. It requires energy and bravery. But once you are aware, you will no longer feel like a cat chasing its tail. Awareness is not fruitless; it allows you to see the things that need to be seen, in yourself and the world around you.

BEING OPEN TO AWARENESS MEANS ACCEPTING THE PAIN AND DISCOMFORT THAT COMES WITH IT.

Awareness sees that you might hurt someone with your words, but it doesn't judge you. It is wise, so it will propel you to go and offer an apology if one is needed.

My friend Annie and I have known each other since we were teenagers – in the days when perms and shoulder pads were cool. (It's a shame this book doesn't have photos in it, otherwise I could show you how cool we looked back then.) The minute we met, we were tight. The quality I adore about this woman, among other things, is her commitment to evolution. She is dedicated to growing, learning and developing. She has also done the work to understand who she is, find her identity and learn to surrender.

Annie's evolution hasn't always been pretty. Understanding yourself and taking responsibility for who you are is often a rocky road. It involves rewriting stories you have told yourself that are not true; asking for forgiveness from others; and forgiving yourself. It's knowing that what you are saying or doing has a ripple effect. Annie does not shy away from that process. She does the work, and she inspires me to do the same. For eight years, with her husband James, she led a church called Encore. Encore's motto was: 'Cheering you on no matter where you are at'. It evolved into a place where their people were encouraged to live in a state of awareness; to accept themselves, and each other, as they are and know that we all have work to do. It was truly an accepting place. (Yes, there are churches that discourage judgement, believe it or not.)

So how do you know if you're in a state of awareness? For me, it's when someone has a differing opinion to me and I recognise the reaction I'm having. Awareness doesn't mean you are no longer of this world and should start wearing a robe or cape. It means you see your fight or flight responses; you are also open to other perspectives; you want to hear others' views, and learn from them and about yourself in the process.

You know you are in awareness when you can see yourself retreating from a situation or conversation and you are driven to question and understand why. It's when you recognise your desire to self-sabotage, yet feel drawn to finding another healthier way.

When you do or say something that doesn't serve you or others and you don't self-assassinate, that's self-awareness. You notice your mistakes, own them without beating yourself up, and learn from them – either at the time, or later. Awareness is cheering yourself on no matter where you are at.

You might ask yourself, 'Why can't I just learn to be a beautiful mess? Why does mess have to be good or bad – why can't it just *be*?' The answer is that the journey to flawsome is not linear. There will be people and areas in your life that will be harder to crack. But moving to a state of awareness and evolution can be only be achieved when, as Plato and Socrates put it, you 'know thyself'.

Your evolution is, simply put, having the courage to be open to another truth. It's to understand that you are perfectly imperfect, and that without an awareness of your flaws you are not being real. Knowing that, awareness breeds evolution.

6

THE PATH TO FLAWSOME

If you are looking for a checklist of things you need to do and say to become flawsome, sorry – I ain't got one. That's because I don't know you. Heck, *you* probably don't even properly know you. But I do have three principles that I have found helpful, gleaned from my more than ten years of studying evolution of self, and the role our reaction to feedback plays in helping us grow.

The feedback you give yourself and the information you gather from those you connect or disconnect with can be used as your superpower. It can help you grow and develop as a leader, a partner, a friend and for yourself. The three components I bring to you here will help you understand how you can learn from every moment, every interaction and every conversation you have with others and yourself. This can set you up for an incredible journey of self-knowing, and ideally self-loving.

THE FEEDBACK YOU GIVE YOURSELF AND THE INFORMATION YOU GATHER FROM THOSE YOU CONNECT OR DISCONNECT WITH CAN BE USED AS YOUR SUPERPOWER.

Will there still be times when you don't like what you see or hear? Yep. Will there still be times when you feel low or inadequate? Probably, because you're human and perfectly flawed. But what I can guarantee is that if you keep getting back up again and continue to apply these three principles, you will get stronger and better each time. I know this because I've done the work myself, and I will keep doing it forever. I am committed to my evolution; it's never-ending.

Let's explore these three principles to go on the ride to becoming flawsome. You will notice they are cyclical: they can happen in order, but are much more likely to happen all at once. However, just like learning a new language, I suggest you start with one thing at a time.

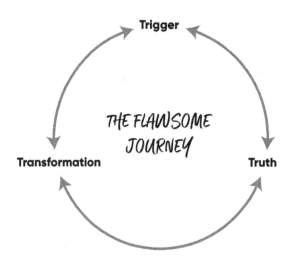

UNDERSTAND YOUR TRIGGERS

Have you ever played a character in a play? Or been in a band, or part of a group presentation? For you to play your role, you would have been looking for a cue from someone else. Whether the cue was a phrase, a look or a movement, you would have waited for it to indicate that it was your turn to play your role.

Identifying the things that trigger you is the same. But if you don't know what to look for, you won't get to learn about the role you play when the trigger occurs; nor will you know how to respond in a way that helps rather than hinders.

In part II of this book we will learn to understand the things that hold us back from staying present, learning and responding in a way that is helpful to ourselves and those around us. Once we know our triggers it's easier to understand how to seek the truth.

SEEK THE TRUTH

The truth is tricky. What's the truth in conversations or situations? Is it what you say, or another person's perspective? Maybe it's a combination of both, or neither.

The reconciliation of what you believe about yourself and the impact you have on others is where you learn. We need to remain open to whatever is coming our way. If we treat feedback as information, the learning begins. When we react poorly, we stifle our opportunity to grow. Your search for truth lies in curiosity and observation.

At a simple level, what you know to be true plus what others know lays the foundation for learning. Learning to meet in the middle and let the truth in (even when it's painful) is where the magic begins. It's fear that holds us back from being open;

fear that what others say or make us feel could be true. In part III we will learn how to seek the truth so we can transform.

CONTINUE YOUR TRANSFORMATION

Transformation sits in courage: your courage to be open to many truths; to know that one perspective of you is just that. It's not automatically adopting others' beliefs, but pondering the information and seeing it as an opportunity to add to what you already know and see. The aim is to add to your pool of truth, not diminish it.

Transformation is endless. It requires discomfort; to know that you are perfectly flawed.

In part IV I will help you see that you are awesome *because* of your flaws – not in spite of them. It's the cracks that make us valuable; it's the flaws that we fill with gold. We just need to learn how.

Your cheat sheet

The journey to being whole is learning to be holey. To make peace with our flaws we need to celebrate them, not hide them. If we honour all of our parts, we can be as we are. Flawsome is the art of seeing our flaws and being awesome because of them, not in spite of them.

We are drawn to people who celebrate their humanity, in all its forms – not their perfection. These people make us feel comfortable to be ourselves. They give us permission to own up to our own flaws. They are more likeable, yet we don't give ourselves this same permission.

We have an unhealthy relationship with feedback. We assume feedback will be bad, so we get on the defensive. We focus on the one piece of negative feedback, even if the rest of it was glowing. We are weird like that.

Feedback is not just found in words and conversations. Feedback is any information that tells you how you feel about something or someone. You could get feedback when you are reading, listening, watching or just thinking. It's information you can learn from, should you choose to see it that way.

Being flawsome starts with *you*. It's not about expecting the world to bend, people to change or circumstances to be different for you to be able to breeze through life. It's about acknowledging that you are reacting in a certain way to things. That's yours to own.

Becoming flawsome requires us to level up. We are in a healthy state when we stay open to and curious about what is going on. This is known as being 'above the line'. We are in an unhelpful and unhealthy state when we have closed, defensive or protective behaviours. This is known as being 'below the line'.

There are five states we can flow through on our journey to flawsome:

1. At our worst we remain trapped in *blame*. Blame is a discharge of truth. It says that someone is wrong (and it's not us) and that we don't need to take responsibility for our reactions. When we blame, we shut ourselves off to possibility and learning. Blame can be aimed outside us at people, groups, circumstances or even systems. It can also be self-directed, which is when we 'should' all over ourselves. Either way it's a form of assassination – of self or others. It keeps us from growing and keeps us below the line.

2. We might be in a place of *denial*. Our fear of reconciling feedback with what we know to be true about ourselves keeps us in our blind spot. In its simplest form, it's a coping mechanism. We are not ready or willing to face what might be true, so we protect ourselves to remain in a perceived 'safe' space. When we stay in this space it creates a disconnection from others and ourselves, as we are holding back parts of ourselves.

3. We start moving above the line when we take *ownership*. Ownership requires a level of self-awareness about the impact you are having on those around you, and yourself. It's about taking responsibility for the good and the bad. We can see when we fall into our fight or flight responses, and accept the impact this has on others – this is the start of self-regulating.

4. In order to move to accepting who we are, we must practise *forgiveness*. Learning to be okay with who we are and where we are at is a significant feat. We are typically tougher on ourselves than we are on others. We don't require others to be perfect or never make mistakes, so we need to learn

to do the same for ourselves. It starts with letting ourselves off the hook and learning from it.

5. To create a place of evolution where we surrender to who we are is when we sit in *awareness*. It's as simple as seeing the truth of what we do, how we think and what we say. That's it. It's observation without the judgement. It's where you learn to be a beautiful mess; to be full of flaws and awesome because of them, not in spite of them. It's seeing your humanity in all its colours and forms.

To move to your flawsome state can be as simple and profound as practising these three principles:

1. Understand your *triggers*. The things that trip you into a state of stress.

2. Seek the *truth*. Know that all perspectives make up what might be true.

3. Continue your *transformation*. Learn that your evolution can happen in the small moments.

PART II

YOUR TRIGGERS

7

LEARN TO LOOK

Ideally, you've now started to identify where you might find yourself in your flawsome journey. You know that some people or circumstances will bring out different reactions in you. You may be able to see that in the past you were in denial, because you've been tapping into your gut a little bit more. Maybe you've recognised that you have been blaming a colleague for their behaviour, and this has been hindering your ability to understand your role in the relationship or circumstance. Or maybe you have taken responsibility for how you come across to others, and committed to learning how to self-manage in these moments. No matter where you are, understanding how you react, or what you react to, in those moments is the first step of understanding your triggers. Good on you!

Every one of us has an inbuilt GPS that can help us understand and navigate the signs of our own evolution. We are wired to self-protect. When we perceive a threat – physical or psychological – our nervous system goes into alert mode. This is not a planned, well-thought-out, deliberate reaction; our body makes a rapid decision and response. Our neurotransmitters and hormones produce changes in our organs; our brain tells our body to create adrenaline and steroids flood into our bloodstream. Then, as we learned about in chapter 5, we can go into fight or flight mode. In circumstances where danger is present this is a good thing. It will give us a surge of adrenaline to remove or protect ourselves from a situation. But when danger is only *perceived*, it's unhelpful.

Threats in your everyday life could include things like:

- approaching a task you have no idea how to do

- being in a social environment you don't feel comfortable in

- public speaking

- hearing feedback about yourself that does not resonate or is hard to hear.

There is no 'danger' in these situations. They might be a threat to your ego or stress levels but they're not life-or-death scenarios. Yet we respond in the same way as we would to a physical threat. You're on high alert and you can respond in unhelpful ways: like going in to fight or flight mode, or simply shutting down.

Fighting is all about winning. You want to 'win' the conversation or situation, so you defend, blame, attack, get personal, talk over, cut off, or use aggressive or passive aggressive tactics – all so you come out on top. In other words, you do all you can to control the situation.

Flighting is all about avoidance. You avoid eye contact, give short responses, even pull out the 'I'm fine' line. (We all know that's code for 'I'm not fine.') You might resort to passive agreement, and do what the other person wants so you can avoid conflict.

Some people may also have a freeze response when they are triggered. Freezing is about shutting down; you just got nothin'. You can't think. You can't speak. You might not even be able to move. You are paralysed by the perceived fear.

These are all just normal human responses when we are under stress.

So how do you know if you are being triggered? The physiological responses are your signs. Your internal radar will warn you that you are about to react in a way that isn't helpful. Your breathing might be elevated; you may become light-headed; you could get tingly fingers or sweaty palms, or even an upset tummy because your digestive system slows down. Your legs and arms may tense up, ready to go into protection mode and to move fast at any moment. Your body will tell you before your brain has worked out what's going on, if you learn to look out for the signs.

SO HOW DO YOU KNOW IF YOU ARE BEING TRIGGERED? THE PHYSIOLOGICAL RESPONSES ARE YOUR SIGNS.

Okay, it's confession time. I, Georgia Murch, know how to be passive aggressive. I know how to give a look that makes the other person feel like they are in the wrong. I know how to ignore someone *just enough* that they are not sure if I am doing it or not. I also know how to give someone a condescending pat or tone of voice so they feel small. In my early years, I wasn't even aware of the damage these behaviours caused. I am now.

When I recognised passive aggression in others, whether they were aware of it or not, I would play the game back. If I were a peacock my feathers would be wide and bright. I would look amazing, but I was playing a game of winning. I would tell myself, 'They shouldn't have done it to me, or others, in the first place. If they hadn't started it, I wouldn't have to respond this way'.

Taking on board another person's emotional state is a thing. It's called an 'emotional transfer'. What a great way to describe the process of taking others' emotions on board. It was Freud who first described this concept of transference as the unconscious redirection of feelings from one person to another. Put simply, it's when you mirror another person's emotional state: they are angry at you, so you become angry; they are upset, so you become upset too; they are frustrated, which causes you to become frustrated. But does the other person really cause it?

It's easy to say, 'I wouldn't be grumpy if you didn't walk around like a crabby sticks in the first place', or, 'I'll be happy when you are'. We can choose to take others' emotions on board, or not. How someone treats you creates a reaction in you, but your reaction is still a choice.

As hard as it is to hear, if we continue to make our emotions a reaction to someone else's we never have to take responsibility for our own. When someone with the flu sneezes on you, your body takes that germ on board. But with emotions, we have a choice to take them on board or not. Making the decision consciously is the start.

IF WE CONTINUE TO MAKE OUR EMOTIONS A REACTION TO SOMEONE ELSE'S, WE NEVER HAVE TO TAKE RESPONSIBILITY FOR OUR OWN.

So next time someone makes you mad, sad or annoyed, ask yourself: 'Have they done this to me, or have I chosen to accept an emotional transfer?' Someone has to stop the transfer – why can't it be you?

CHOOSE KINDNESS

If you've ever been to a developing country, you'll know life is very different to our protected, lucky life in the Western world. You can't drink the tap water, be guaranteed an education or have your medical needs met. We take so much for granted in Western countries.

Often if you're visiting developing countries you can rent a bike, car or scooter with no experience. You will probably find yourself sharing a very skinny dirt road with other people, cats, dogs and even ducks. So who owns the road? Who's the king that we all need to move to the side for? They all are. No-one is more important than another; they have orderly chaos.

You will probably find if you step in front of a bike or car you don't get tooted. (Well, not aggressively, anyway.) If you pull out on your scooter in front of a car or person, no-one gives you the bird. (Well, an Aussie might, but certainly no locals do.) Why is this?

You are not given a rule book about how to drive in these countries. Often there are not even road signs. There are very few traffic lights, even on busy intersections. So how is order kept? How do tempers remain low?

Well, it's because the road is not ruled by rules; it's governed by kindness.

Kindness doesn't crack the s★★ts when someone pulls out in front.

Kindness doesn't take poor indication personally.

Kindness doesn't behave like the most important person on the road.

You know what kindness does?

Kindness lets people in.

Kindness works out how to go with the flow.

Kindness knows that together we can make it work.

Kindness is a culture, made up of individuals. It's not a system.

Thich Nhat Hanh, the famous Vietnamese monk, gives us a beautiful way to think about things when someone tries to cause us harm:

When another person makes you suffer, it is because he suffers deeply within himself, and his suffering is spilling over. He does not need punishment; he needs help. That's the message he is sending.

So the next time you crack it at the person in the coffee shop, or get grumpy with an Uber driver or triggered off in the car by someone you've never met, you get to decide. What would kindness do? Blame would say the other person shouldn't have said or done that; that the other person needs to be faster, instead of you learning to be more patient. Blame would make the other person the problem, which means that you don't need to look at your own behaviour.

BLAME IS EASY, AND IT MEANS YOU STAY TRAPPED.

Blame is easy, and it means you stay trapped. So, don't ask the world to be kinder. Remember: *you* are the world. *You* are the people. *You* are the one who can make a brighter day. So, let's start giving.

(Yeah, I may have pulled that last bit from the lyrics to 'We Are the World'. But my point is made.) Choose kindness. It starts in the small moments.

STAY ABOVE THE LINE

We learned about being 'above the line' or 'below the line' in chapter 5. Being above the line rather than below it is the difference between being the victim or the victor. As a victim, you are not in control and your responses are whatever you feel at the time. As a victor, you are *choosing* a better response. You are being strong.

When you are above the line you are open-minded, curious to know more and committed to learning – about yourself and others. If you're above the line, you believe that learning and growing are more important than being right. When you are below the line, you are closed or defensive. Keep in mind we can oscillate above or below the line at any time based on the situation we are in, people we are with, content we are consuming or our physical state.

Let's look at some examples of responses above and below the line.

Patience, tolerance, kindness, curiosity, openness, commitment, understanding, forgiveness, ownership, accountability, seeking solutions, making choices, finding better ways and seeking and giving feedback.

Above the line

Blame, denial, sarcasm, envy, jealousy, greed, grudges, gossip, avoidance, combative behaviour, hate, resentment, excuses, ignoring, seeking out problems, finding fault, 'stuckness' and annoyance.

Below the line

Our humanity means we often fall into both categories. That's what makes us flawsome. So when you're considering these responses, no self-punishment, please – just observation.

Here's the thing about observation. The simple act of seeing things, observing them and being mindful of them often leads to change. Just noticing that you are doing things or thinking things means your brain can review and rewire to change your response in the future. Observation helps you to notice (even subconsciously) that you are about to do something that you now know is below the line. Over time it creates a bigger gap between the trigger and your response time. Good, right?

THE SIMPLE ACT OF SEEING THINGS, OBSERVING THEM AND BEING MINDFUL OF THEM OFTEN LEADS TO CHANGE.

Psychiatrist Judson Brewer has shown us that simply being mindful of, and curious about our triggers and behaviour, is enough for us to become wise. When we are wise, we can respond in different ways to our triggers.

In his book *The Power of Habit,* Charles Duhigg tells us about a weight loss study conducted in 2009. For at least one day per week, obese participants were asked to record what they ate. It took a little time for people to remember their food diaries and record all their snacks, but they got there. Some decided to start recording more days, and for many this process of recording became a habit.

Then something unexpected happened: the habit of recording their food helped the participants to see eating patterns they were not aware of before. Six months down the track, the people who had adopted the one simple habit of recording their food daily had lost twice as much weight as those who hadn't. No specific actions were taken: they just saw the data, and made changes as a result.

So, if we just start observing our reactions and behaviours, we will start to notice them before we fall into the trap of unhelpful behaviours. How powerful is that?

I love Michelle Obama's perspective on responding to our triggers: 'When someone is cruel or acts like a bully, you don't stoop to their level. No, our motto is, "When they go low, we go high"'. She sees it with this clarity; that's why we only see her grace. After reading her autobiography *Becoming* I am majorly crushing on her, like millions of others I know.

CAN YOU FEEL IT?

There is a rare condition called congenital insensitivity or analgesia. It's where your body can't feel physical pain. You could put your hand on a stove or break your leg and you wouldn't feel it. We can all suffer from a form of this when it comes to connecting to our triggers. Someone's words may have hurt us in the past, but we have desensitised ourselves to the pain because it's too much to cope with. We may hear ourselves saying things like:

'Doesn't bother me!'

'I don't care.'

'It's not an issue.'

'That's just their stuff.'

'It's not my problem.'

You may believe these statements to be true, but they are all defensive responses. They keep you from connecting with how you really feel.

DEFENSIVE RESPONSES KEEP YOU FROM CONNECTING WITH HOW YOU REALLY FEEL.

If you're a fan of *Game of Thrones* (if not, download immediately – it's amazing) you will know the character called Bran Stark. He is the fourth child of the Starks who ruled a region called Winterfell. When he was six years old, he was pushed from a high window and woke up after being in a coma unable to walk, ever again. During his slumber he received an amazing gift: the ability to view humanity's collective memories. All of what we see in our life, he would now see – past, present and future. Now that's a lot of stuff to process; the good and the bad.

In order to cope with the volume of joy and pain that his mind could now hold, Bran shut down emotionally. He had no fear, no happiness, no sorrow.

In the final season (don't worry, not much of a spoiler alert) when Theon was protecting him from the Night King, he tells him not to be afraid. Bran responds with, 'I don't feel anymore'. He's like a zombie: alive but without feeling. The lights are on, but no-one is home. The only way for him to have survived this far was to shut down his emotional state so he could cope with the information he had.

We can have a touch of the Bran Starks. (Not the seeing all, knowing all bit – actually, let's be honest, some of us think we have that power.) I'm talking about the bit where we shut down our emotions in order to cope with our past. We numb ourselves so we don't have to experience the pain of memories or emotions.

The thing is: if you can't see or feel it, how can you ever deal with it? We need to 'learn to look' for how we are responding to others. We talked about finding the gold in difficult situations in chapter 4, and it can be the same with our triggers. You must choose to look and be brave enough to take ownership of what triggers you, in order to heal from it.

For a long time, I was triggered when people told me I was controlling or that I needed to have things my way. Once I moved past being dismissive or even annoyed by the feedback, I learned to see it. It hurt knowing that people saw me that way, and that I actually *was* being that way. But once I dared to look, knowing my trigger was a little piece of gold that helped me take ownership and grow.

Our challenge is to be brave; brave enough to look for our triggers and own them, and not numb ourselves to the feelings that result. They might be exactly what we need to understand so we can move to being flawsome.

OUR CHALLENGE IS TO BE BRAVE; BRAVE ENOUGH TO LOOK FOR OUR TRIGGERS AND OWN THEM, AND NOT NUMB OURSELVES TO THE FEELINGS THAT RESULT.

8

REACTIONS ARE CHOICES

I grew up in Melbourne, Australia. My city is known for having 'four seasons in one day'. It's true: we can literally go from 45 to 18 degrees Celsius within an hour. Being prepared is key. It's a bit like us humans: we can go from hot to cold in a matter of seconds. We need to be prepared for this, just like we need to bring an umbrella in case of unexpected rain. We also need an emotional umbrella to help us take shelter from the things that upset us and we want to react to.

My good friend, psychologist and expert in interpersonal safety Dr Amy Silver, says, 'We need to create the conditions for our own psychological safety. When we feel safe, we can slow down our brain's hardwiring for defensiveness'. I love this; she's saying that we have the power to create the conditions – in ourselves – to choose how we respond to our triggers.

We all know that when we are in conversations, or just doing life in general, the only person we can control is ourself – right? So this is where we are going to start, and finish. There is no magic wand to change the people or environment around you.

You can influence; you can make decisions about minimising time with people or situations that trigger you; but you can't control other people. Bummer, right?

THERE IS NO MAGIC WAND TO CHANGE THE PEOPLE OR ENVIRONMENT AROUND YOU.

For those of us who have an 'interesting' relationship with control, that can be quite confronting. I can often measure where I am at, in myself, by my yoga practice – particularly when I practise with others. I know something is up if I'm focusing on the room being too hot or too cold; the teacher talking too softly or too much; the class not being 'power flow' enough, or too fast. As soon as I am getting frustrated, annoyed or wanting the teacher to do it a better way (which is code for 'my way'), I know I am not taking responsibility for the role I am playing in the situation. In other words, I'm not taking responsibility for how I am choosing to react. Yes, the teacher could change the class to suit what I need, but what about the rest of the yogis in the room? Is that what they want? Who knows, because I am making it all about me.

What about when you're with someone who is clearly not being respectful, towards you or others? It may be your passive aggressive work colleague who loves pulling out an eye roll when they disagree with you or others, or your friend who gets upset when you try to talk them through something that's important to you. Or your kids, or partner, who nag and whinge and demand things of you. Even listening to someone speak poorly about another person fits in to this category (it's code for gossip). Well, I've got some good news for you. When we are in situations that we don't like or with people who challenge us, we can take control back. Yep, we can take things into our own hands. And by things, I mean our reactions. How we respond is our choice, whether it feels that way or not. It starts with you.

BE CAREFUL OF THE DRAMA TRAP

When I was a teenager my mum always used to call me a drama queen. I never knew what it meant, but I knew from her tone that she didn't appreciate it. All I knew was that I felt emotional, and she wasn't having a bar of it.

So, when I heard of the drama triangle, created by psychotherapist Stephen Karpman, I was all ears. Now I use it as a way of determining where I am contributing, or helping others to identify their role in situations. I've come to realise that some of the less-than-favourable scenarios in my life were actually being allowed, supported and – at worst – started by me.

Maybe you can think of a couple of scenarios right now that are causing you stress or anxiety, or some conversations you've been having that feel heavy. People who identify with any of the roles in the drama triangle create dysfunction for themselves and those around them. According to Karpman, there are three roles we can play:

1. **The victim.** The victim sees themselves as powerless. Victims often feel helpless and hopeless. The victim believes they are not able to change their negative circumstances and are not open to believing they have the power to change them. They deny any responsibility for their role – even allowing or enabling their own situation. They often hold back and won't stand their ground. They can be very sensitive, have a 'poor me' mentality and feel like others are

against them. They will look for a 'rescuer' that will support their perspective. If the victim stays in this role, they are not able to progress their thinking or decision-making.

2. **The rescuer.** The rescuer sees themselves as the hero. They come from a place of wanting to help the situation, or the victim, so they step in to 'help'. They are often tired and have physical complaints because they neglect their own needs to solve other people's issues. Rescuers may be loud or have a quiet, martyr style. They can 'feel bad' if they don't rescue others, and can keep the victim dependent. They create unhealthy co-dependent relationships, as this plays to their ego and need to be needed. They have a motive, seen or unseen, to feel better as a person.

3. **The perpetrator.** The perpetrator sees themselves as a 'reformer' because they are pushing things or people forward. They pressure, coerce or persecute the victim. They blame the victim and criticise the behaviour of the rescuer, without providing guidance, assistance or a solution to the underlying problem. They can be highly critical and good at finding fault. Perpetrators often feel inadequate underneath. They control with threats, order and rigidity. They can be loud or quiet in style, and can sometimes be bullies. They can be the 'critical' parent or boss. They tend to spread rumours and gossip about others.

So have a think about the things that keep you awake at night or even the relationships that irritate you. Are you trapped in your own drama triangle? Have you just had that moment when you realise there are things in your life that cause you stress or anxiety (big or small), and you are enabling or even igniting them?

The cool thing about the drama triangle is that it can become a diagnostic for you to see where you might be stuck in your own evolution. When we are traumatised, from the past or the present, we can stay trapped – often waiting for those around us who have wronged us to fix the situation.

THE DRAMA TRIANGLE CAN BECOME A DIAGNOSTIC FOR YOU TO SEE WHERE YOU MIGHT BE STUCK IN YOUR OWN EVOLUTION.

I love Will Smith's take on the difference between fault and responsibility. He says, 'It doesn't matter whose fault it is that something is broken. But it's your responsibility to fix it'. It could even be you who is a little broken, right? It wasn't your fault that you had an abusive parent. But dealing with the impact it has on you and those around you is your responsibility. It's not your fault if your partner cheated on you and ruined your marriage, or if your co-workers are difficult to deal with. But if you give the person who wronged you the responsibility of fixing it, you are giving over your power. Others can't fix your heart, your happiness and your life; that's your gig. It's not fair, but that's how it rolls.

As long you are pointing the finger at other people, you are stuck; you can't move forward. It's like drinking a bottle of poison in the hope it will kill your enemies. You're not admitting any responsibility. Remember that responsibility is not about letting others off the hook: it's about you stepping up and taking your power back.

Until you accept what's happening or happened to you, you will remain in drama.

So why are we talking about drama and the things that keep us trapped? Because being trapped will hold us back from being present with others and from learning about ourselves. It means we limit the potential of our relationships, our career and ourselves. We need to identify when we are triggered and trapped, and take responsibility for our reactions, otherwise we can't fix things or grow.

UNTIL YOU ACCEPT WHAT'S HAPPENING OR HAPPENED TO YOU, YOU WILL REMAIN IN DRAMA.

9

WHAT ARE YOUR TRIGGERS?

Let's try to understand specifically what revs us into fight, flight or freeze mode; what triggers our nervous system so we react rather than stay present; and what keeps us trapped in the drama triangle.

But before we start, it's important to note that not all triggers are bad. Some of them help to guide us and inspire us into healthy action.

When I led HR for a management consultancy firm, every six months we had a People Capital meeting with our management team. The purpose of this meeting was to gather feedback from the leaders about the performance and development of people on projects and in their roles. We would use this information to give staff members a ranking which would affect their bonus and/or career development within the firm, in a positive or negative way. These meetings were really important to my team, and I loved them as well. I enjoyed hearing about the evolution of our people or what they needed to be able to grow.

I distinctly remember my first People Capital meeting. One of our project directors – we'll call him Richard – came to give feedback on one of his team members. He said that she was good with clients but wasn't great when it came to organisation. She was fantastic as a facilitator but her design skills were poor. There were some clear divides and strong opinions. So I asked Richard, 'What did she say when you gave her this feedback?'. His response? Crickets.

He hadn't told her. I could feel my frustration rising. We were going to make a decision about someone's career without giving her the chance to understand and improve, or even to see whether what we were saying was fair. This seemed really wrong, and unfair. So I told him so. (Not one of my finest examples on how to give someone feedback about their feedback, since I said it in front of his peers and in frustration. Ah, the irony, right?)

It was from here that my quest to understand how to give and receive feedback – in a way that builds trust and respect – started. And three books later, here I am. Do you see my point? My frustration, my trigger, became my cause. My sense of injustice propelled me into positive action. My trigger also propelled me into an unhealthy response. Instead of leading a conversation, I made it an accusation. Accusations aren't inspiring or relationship-building; in fact, they can have the opposite effect.

Here, we are going to focus on the triggers that help us understand *ourselves*. They are a flag for something that is affecting us. You've probably heard the saying, 'The problem is not the real problem'. This means that we react and solve the presenting issue – not the underlying one. Like when someone puts a cup down loudly on the table, and you jolt and get a fright and ask them to be quieter – but it could be that you are just on edge because of something else that is going on. Or you might like

Jack Sparrow's version from *Pirates of the Caribbean*: 'The problem is not the problem. The problem is your attitude about the problem'. It could be that how we are seeing something is making it worse. It's the same for when we are triggered.

WE REACT AND SOLVE THE PRESENTING ISSUE – NOT THE UNDERLYING ONE.

The issue might not be the issue. It's just triggering something deeper.

Think of things that are frustrating you at the moment. It doesn't matter what or who they are – just get them in your mind. You can look at these in the context of understanding your triggers to see if you have particular patterns you fall into.

When we are not awake to the things that trigger us, we stay trapped in our automatic responses. When we recognise them, we can self-manage and reset. We all have things that can set us off. Sometimes we can anticipate them before we've even spoken to the other person and other times they rush in like a tornado. So, what's it all about? What holds us back from keeping the conversation flowing like a well-rehearsed dance?

In their book *Thanks for the Feedback*, Douglas Stone and Sheila Heen tell us we have triggers that hold us back from 'finding the gold' in the conversations or feedback moments. Yet triggers are not reserved for conversations alone; they can also happen in circumstances. So, let's look at six triggers that create our stress reactions; six things that hold us back from listening, understanding and learning from the other person, whether you believe there is something to learn or not.

1. WE HAVE A 'CONTENT' TRIGGER

This is when the other person's truth is not our truth; when we are set off by the content itself. It's when we don't like what is being said or shown because we think it's untrue, unfair or unhelpful. As a result, we feel wronged, resentful and frustrated. It might be that another person is sharing their opinions or feelings and they don't resonate with you; or that someone has made assumptions about you, your character or the circumstance that are not true or unfair.

When I was told I could be intimidating it did not resonate with me. I did not connect with the content. Their opinion was not my opinion, so I chose not to find the learning. What's something that someone has said about you that you didn't care to understand or look into? A good friend of mine called me a tightarse the other day – this is the complete opposite of how I see myself. Yet when he gave a couple of examples, I could see why he thought that. He had a different interpretation of the word than I did, but he helped me see how it could be perceived that way. It was painful, but useful.

If you value data and evidence this could be your trigger. If someone shares information that you believe is incorrect – let's call it 'fake news' – then you could be triggered. It becomes an opinion war, or you opt out of communicating. But remember: even if they are wrong, we have a choice about how we respond.

2. WE HAVE A 'RELATIONSHIP' TRIGGER

Sometimes you might find yourself having a reaction to the person sharing the content, feedback or information. You might have a history with that person, putting the relationship on shaky ground; or you might have heard things about them, from others, that cause you to put your guard up. It might be that they don't lead by example, they have no credibility or that you simply don't like or respect them. In these situations, we can start to focus on the audacity of the person sharing this content with us.

Relationship triggers are often the easiest to spot. It could be an ex-friend or ex-lover and your history and experience with them means you are triggered even when you see their name coming up on your phone or hear them mentioned in conversation with others. It could be someone you work with whose character or personality don't seem to offer you much; before they even speak you have decided whatever they are about to say won't be worth listening to. It could be a public figure whose views you don't share, so you automatically discount what they have to say – often before they've even spoken.

I remember when my good friend told me that our mutual friend (let's call her Jane) had said some stuff about me. My friend was letting me know so I was aware of what was being said when I wasn't in the room. It was about my character, and it wasn't 100 per cent kind. How do you think I went the next time I saw Jane? Did I want to let her know exactly what I was thinking (that admittedly was below the line)? Damn straight I did. But I also wanted to live a life being proud of who I am, what I do and what I say. I chose to work on staying open and tried not to judge her. We all have triggers – it's what we do with them that counts. (In this example I had a relationship *and* a content trigger: I didn't agree with what was being said, *and* I now struggled with her on a relationship level.)

I did have a conversation with her about what I had heard (with my friend's permission to share, of course). It ended up being a super-cool convo about how we impact each other; a much better outcome than if I had simply spoken my mind.

Crazy that tough conversations can actually make situations better, right?

3. WE HAVE AN 'IDENTITY' TRIGGER

This trigger is about your ego being challenged. It's when your reaction is not about the content or the person, but about how the information challenges your sense of self and who you believe you are. You feel overwhelmed, threatened or ashamed. You get off-balance and question yourself, and this is not a happy place – so you react rather than listen and try to understand.

Ego is big; it's a whole book in itself. The ego is the part of yourself that you show the world. It's the surface part of your personality; the 'game face' you wear because you don't want to let people see who you really are. Our ego helps us make sense of ourselves and who we believe we are. It's our identity.

Yet it also holds us back from learning about the parts of ourselves that we don't like. It prevents us from being vulnerable and truly honest with ourselves and those around us about the parts of ourselves that we're not proud of.

Your ego will not want to hear that you are not perfect, not pretty enough, not strong enough, not smart enough, not kind enough, not thoughtful, not a good enough friend or partner. It's because you can't reconcile what they're saying with who you are – so you blame the other person or get triggered off.

UNLESS I AM PREPARED TO SEE MY FLAWS, I WILL STAY AS I AM.

My ego does not want to hear that my keynote could have been better, or that when I swear I upset people, or that I could have handled a parenting situation better. It really doesn't. But unless I am prepared to see my flaws, I will stay as I am.

Here's one way to work out if you have identity triggers. If you no longer had your career, or were no longer a parent (let's not imagine you don't have kids at all, but maybe that you are no longer their primary caregiver), or were not part of the event or club you attend, how would you feel? A little lost?

It might be that your identity is caught up in what you do, not who you are; that you identify with the role you play, rather than your character. You believe you are only worth something when you are playing that role. When you perceive someone having a jab at your ability to do that role, boom! Trigger in action.

4. WE HAVE A 'DELIVERY' TRIGGER

This one is all about *how* the information is delivered. Being a feedback expert, I see a lot of this. It's not about the words or the person; it's about how something is said, where it's said and when. Often the delivery trigger occurs when feedback is delivered in a harsh or disrespectful way, or in front of others. It could be delivered via text or email when the honourable thing would be to do it in person or over the phone. We all know someone who has broken up with their significant other via text, right? In this type of situation, we often become incensed with how the message is delivered rather than the message itself.

Sometimes apologies are given many months after an issue occurred, and instead of focusing on the content of the message we are triggered by how late it is. Or we could react to someone giving us feedback straight after something when we weren't ready. Either way, it's the delivery that sets us off, rather than the message.

How people speak to me is a trigger for me. If it's aggressive or passive aggressive I can feel my heart start pumping. This is my sign that I am being triggered. The other one is when people talk *at* me, rather than *with* me. I'm sure you know people who love the sound of their own voice more than anything; you might as well not be there. The other day a student at my yoga class was talking non-stop (I'm not exaggerating) for 11 minutes before the class started. She described what she'd been doing, how her practice is going, how her health is – all with the volume of a megaphone. She didn't ask one question or listen to others. I had to breathe. I got triggered and she wasn't even talking to me.

When it comes to preparing for feedback moments, I know this: people hear your content, and smell your intent. What I mean is that the words are important, but it's the intent behind what people are saying that we more often get triggered by. It's why you sometimes feel confused in moments when people are saying the right thing but it doesn't feel genuine; your gut is telling you that something is off.

PEOPLE HEAR YOUR CONTENT, AND SMELL YOUR INTENT.

The point is, if it's the way things are being said, and where and when, that sets you off – that's a delivery trigger.

5. WE HAVE AN 'INJUSTICE' TRIGGER

The injustice trigger is all about our sense of fairness: what's right and wrong. Why do the people who really deserve the promotion (this might include you) not receive one? Why do the bullies get away with their behaviour? Why does one person get paid more than another? Why does one person's history not get exposed but yours does? Why do we treat one race better than another? Injustice is when things don't feel fair – and sometimes they are not.

Injustice can also be something that spurs us on for the greater good. It creates campaigns that push change such as same-sex marriage, or the protection of animals. It helps us move the dial on global conversations such as climate change. On a personal note, it can spur us into action to have the conversation that gets us a pay rise or teaches a kid how to stand up to bullies, or even protect a stranger from someone speaking to them poorly.

A sense of injustice is a trigger; how we respond can be above or below the line. The climate change debate is a current example. If you believe we are not doing enough, that can be a trigger; if you think we are wasting time on the debate, that can also be a trigger. Either way, how are you responding? Are you annoyed, angry or blameful? Or are you open-minded, curious and willing to push forward with kindness?

If Nelson Mandela had been triggered off every time people were against equality, would he have toppled apartheid? If Rosie Batty had cracked it at everyone who said women ask to be beaten by staying in relationships, do you think people would have listened to her as much? I don't think so. These people acknowledged we don't all think the same and that education, above the line, is key.

6. WE HAVE AN 'INCOMPETENCE' TRIGGER

This trigger is about the value we place on others' capability. Most of you have heard people say, 'I don't suffer fools'. It's another way of saying, 'I don't tolerate stupidity, or people who are slow or don't think the way I think they should'. I hear it a lot. I get it.

Working or hanging out with people who are 'slow thinkers' or make ridiculous comments or come to dumb conclusions can be super-frustrating. I am the first to see how this can grate on you. But how we treat them is our responsibility, and this trigger is grounded in judgement.

You may be surprised to hear that the phrase to 'suffer fools' is very old. It was, in fact, first coined more than 2000 years ago by Saint Paul in a letter he wrote to a church in Corinth. Paul said, 'Suffer fools gladly'. He was saying that we need to be open to people who are of a 'lesser mind'; we should treat them with respect and do the honourable thing.

Our modern version of this saying has turned it around and gives us permission to avoid putting up with people who we feel are not as smart or good as us. Some people wear this phrase as a badge of honour. I don't think there's much honour in it at all.

To become frustrated or dismissive of people you believe to be stupid is unhelpful and below the line. I love and resonate with Simon Sinek's perspective:

If you want to be a great leader, remember to treat all people with respect at all times. For one, because you never know when you'll need their help. And two, because it's a sign you respect people, which all great leaders do.

There are some amazing people in this world who have influence in a healthy way by treating people with respect at all times. I love watching Barack Obama, or his wife Michelle, in action. You don't hear them, or Oprah, or Richard Branson putting people down.

Yes, people can slow success down, be frustrating to work with and, at worst, get their stupid on. But treating them with disrespect is not the solution. If you do so, you are now the lesser version of yourself.

THE WAY PEOPLE TREAT YOU IS A MEASURE OF THEIR CHARACTER. HOW YOU RESPOND IS A MEASURE OF YOURS.

I believe that the way people treat you is a measure of their character. How you respond is a measure of yours. If we always make the other person the problem, we never take responsibility for the role we play or how we treat them. That's not okay; it's blaming them for who they are, and giving ourselves permission to get off scot-free. 'It's not my fault they are so stupid' is a cop out.

Compassion should win, not your ego. That's how you become the person that others want to work with and be with. I'm not saying it's easy, but it's a better intent than blame. We don't grow if we are in blame.

If you have an incompetence trigger, then know that it's yours. What can you learn from it?

SO, WHAT ARE *YOUR* TRIGGERS?

If you make a list of the things that trigger you, you might start to see a pattern. Are many of your triggers content triggers, where you are seeking truth? Are most of them injustice triggers, when things are not fair?

Sometimes the reason these triggers are challenging is not that they are untruthful or even unreasonable, but because they pull us away from our own awareness. If we are triggered, we can stop learning to look for the lesson (or the gold) in the situation. We become trapped in drama and our stress responses and we are no longer listening – we are reacting. In these situations we will always find an excuse to avoid accepting what is being shared with us.

Triggers are the reason why we don't run around asking everyone for feedback, and we avoid spending time with some people or reading articles that we might be offended by. The challenge is to look to see if our triggers are present, and own the fact that we are triggered.

As soon as you can see yourself falling into a stress response you can be sure you're triggered by something. In the moment, it doesn't matter what the trigger is; the bit you want to be conscious of is staying connected to yourself so you can see your reactions. You can take control of yourself and, over time, learn to respond in a way that creates growth.

10

WHERE DO TRIGGERS COME FROM?

Here's the big question: where the hell do our triggers come from? Why can one person be spoken to in exactly the same way you were, and you struggle with it but they don't? Why can one person read a news story about injustice and not be affected, while others are seething?

I'm going to try to answer a complex question with a simple answer. All your life experiences (nurture) and the person who are you are at the core (nature) influence what you believe about life, others and yourself.

MY NURTURE INFLUENCES WHO I AM

Paul was my first-ever boyfriend, at age 14. I found out he was pashing my best friend Anne behind my back, and I was crushed – I mean seriously devo. When she told me, it literally felt like a knife to the guts. After that experience, I was nervous that all boys would cheat; I even treated them as though they would. I was slow to trust, and I'm sure I pushed several away because of my insecurities.

My life experience was that Paul cheated on me. My belief became that boys could cheat on me. My actions were to treat boys with mistrust and their words as suspicious. I now know that my experience with Paul does not apply to others. Every situation is different.

Every experience you do or don't have can end up defining how you feel and what you believe. Here are some of the things that can impact your attitudes and beliefs. (A strong note: this list is not comprehensive, and I'm not saying these statements are necessarily true for you. Treat this as a starting point to get yourself thinking about how your experiences might have shaped you.) Impactful experiences could include:

- **Parenting.** The type of parents you have (or didn't have) affects you. It could be that you had an absent parent, which meant you had to look after yourself because no-one else was there to do it. An overprotective parent could mean that you didn't have to deal with issues yourself, so resilience has not been a learned skill. You could have had parents who gave you a great sense of self and affirmed you and how important you are; or they could have done the opposite, so your self-worth is low.

- **Community.** The people around you will affect your values. What they believe and the actions they take can become your norm. If you have spent time with people who love to gossip, you are likely to become focused on others rather than yourself. Negativity and judgement can become your norm. If you are with people who focus on caring for others, you will believe in the good of others.

- **Bullying.** If you have experienced bullying at school, home or work it can have a profound effect on your self-belief. If others had significant control over you in your junior years, you might react by trying to control as much of your life as you can (and perhaps those around you).

▶ **Spiritual.** Your religious or spiritual upbringing, or recent experiences, will influence what you believe and how you judge yourself and others. Spiritual experiences can give you a sense of what is right and what is wrong, or of life being black and white. You might have more compassion as a result, or less; you might judge more, or less. It depends on your experiences.

▶ **Trauma.** Trauma will have a significant impact on your beliefs about yourself and the world around you. It could create fear about certain types of people, travelling or places. Trauma is not something you asked for, but it is something that needs to be processed. It could mean it's harder for you to trust people, or to trust in a higher power or the Universe. It could be that you self-protect so you don't have to experience pain again.

▶ **Death or illness.** This can impact you whether it involves people you are close to, or it has affected people you 'do life' with. Sometimes we can even be affected by death or illness in people we have never met. Of course, you could also be suffering from illness yourself, whether it's a once-off or recurring issue. The thought of going to the doctor could be enough to set you off.

▶ **Safety.** When your physical or psychological safety is threatened or breached it can put you on permanent alert. It can create barriers that mean you might not put yourself out there to have experiences with people or places because you may expect the same thing to happen.

Most of our reactions come from the stories or assumptions we create from deep within. American psychologist Abraham Maslow would say we react when our needs are not being met. (Remember learning about Maslow's hierarchy of needs at school?) Sebastian Junger, author of *Tribe*, would say that our need to belong is greater than our need for safety, water and even food. So would my friend Michelle Loch, who is an expert in the role neuroscience plays in leadership. Our need to belong is big. When we don't feel a sense of belonging, it has a significant impact.

What that means is that if our need to be loved, cared about or even listened to has not been met at times throughout our life, this will have had an impact. Our brains process this in whatever way they can, and we then live out of these stories and will react to them, until we understand our triggers. This is why we need to be careful about the stories we tell ourselves; we see people and situations through our own life filters. Our experiences dictate how we view the world.

WE NEED TO BE CAREFUL ABOUT THE STORIES WE TELL OURSELVES; WE SEE PEOPLE AND SITUATIONS THROUGH OUR OWN LIFE FILTERS.

Men with big egos used to trigger me. Sometimes I would be in a meeting and I could practically smell one walking into the room. I could see their puffed-out chests. They would talk over the top of everyone because no-one's opinion mattered except their own. I would feel my jaw tensing and my hands clenching in response. Sometimes I would even role-play some one-liners in my head to put big-ego men back in their box. You know what that ended up being about? My dad issues. I didn't feel seen by my dad, so I projected my feelings on to men like him. While it is our parents' job to make us feel safe and valued, it isn't a role they always play. It's not fair, but that's what happens. Helping me understand the impact my relationship with my dad has had on me, and forgiving him, created the shift I needed. Men with big egos no longer trigger me. You won't always find such strong correlations in every trigger, but your reactions will always have a meaning behind them – if you dare to look for it.

I've also noticed that when I feel like people talk *at* me, that's about *my need* to be seen. When others talk, and don't ask me questions, I don't feel heard. I've learnt that I was taking others personally and it wasn't about them. It was about me.

What life experiences have you had that may have influenced what you believe about yourself or the world around you? What has happened to you that has dictated a false belief? You will always find answers. It's just having the courage to look for them.

YOU CAN'T ESCAPE YOUR DNA

Half of your DNA comes from your mum and half from your dad. Sorry – it's a genetic fact. For some of us this is good news. For others, it's something we would like to stay in denial about. (Or just be peed off about.) Some of you might not even know who your parents are. We all have a story, right?

I was forever trying to undo 'The Murch' in me – the component that felt like it was stuck to me with superglue. I was too bossy. Too opinionated. Too direct. Too 'Murch'. I always felt like I was fighting against something out of my control. But was I? And did I need to fight against it?

Many years ago, I was at an all-time low. I found myself in a dysfunctional relationship. It was slowly eating away at my sense of self, my energy and my physical and psychological health. I lost a lot of weight and anxiety was my permanent companion. Then the relationship ended, and my health deteriorated further. I had a couple of 'episodes' that we now recognise as transient ischaemic attacks (TIAs; in other words, small strokes). My mental health was affecting my physical self, and I was struggling to be present. After a day or, sometimes, even an hour with clients I would spend the next 24 hours in bed. I was spent.

During this time it felt like everything was triggering me. I would have to self-manage to avoid crying at the drop of a hat, and hold back from telling people what I really thought of them. I wanted to transfer my pain on to others. (Not that I knew that at the time.) I didn't know how I would come back, but I realised my game face would only last so long. I was running the business so I had to keep going. I had to find a way.

Enter Alessandra Edwards. Author of *The DNA of Performance*, Alessandra is an expert in helping people unlock their genetic and biological potential and I bloody love her! I just knew she was someone who could help me get back on track. We did lots of tests to understand how my body was performing (or not, in this case). The DNA test was the most interesting for me. It looked at my genes, my biomechanics and how I am made up, and I worked with Alessandra to figure out how to play to that to get the best out of who I am. Fast forward six months and I had no more fuzzy brain, temper tantrums or tears. I felt strong-bodied and clear-minded. Working with her was a game changer.

**I AM THE WAY I AM.
THE BEST THING TO DO IS TO
WORK WITH IT – NOT AGAINST IT.**

Alessandra helped me understand that how I am wired affects how I do life. Yes, there are things I can influence and even control, but there are others I can't. I am the way I am. The best thing to do is to work with it – not against it.

In *The DNA of Performance*, Alessandra says:

The variations that are found in our DNA – which make us a one-of-a-kind, never-to-be-reproduced-ever-again individual – interact differently with external environmental triggers to make some people more resilient 'warriors' and others more emotionally in-tune 'worriers'.

So, based on our nature and nurture, we respond in ways that are unique to us. This is important to recognise and take responsibility for.

When we are low in energy we fight or flight more easily. This happens on two levels. First, we are triggered more easily. Our body is already stressed so our defences are down. We may read into things more than we normally would. Things that we would normally let slide or not affect us start to grate or upset us. Second, our self-control is harder to manage as well. Our natural response to stress is elevated.

Your nurture experiences will affect what you believe and how you behave; your nature will influence how you respond to stress. Understanding both helps you level up. It also gives you permission to be flawsome. That's what life gave you so let's work with it, not against it.

11

WHEN STALLING IS
A GOOD THING

Have you ever walked away from a conversation and five minutes later you think, 'I could have said XYZ'. Grrr. Or maybe you have what I call 'regretitis': where you are in the middle of a conversation and you think, 'I wish I didn't say XYZ'.

We all have fight and flight responses that we regret or wish we could have done better. Our triggers cause us to react, and our reactions don't often help.

As I said in chapter 9, the reason these triggers are challenging us is not that they are untruthful or even unreasonable. It's because they pull us away from our own awareness. They stop us from learning to look and find the lesson or the gold in the situation. We are trapped in drama and our stress responses, and we are no longer listening – we are reacting. We find an excuse not to accept what is being shared with us.

Our triggers are the reason why we don't run around asking everyone for feedback. The challenge is to look to see if our triggers are present and own the fact that we are choosing not to respond well.

OUR TRIGGERS ARE THE REASON WHY WE DON'T RUN AROUND ASKING EVERYONE FOR FEEDBACK.

Author and researcher Brené Brown tells us that when we feel backed into a corner we typically have one of three reactions:

1. we run

2. we please our way out of it

3. we come out swinging.

When you think you are in danger of saying or doing something you might regret, I propose you do something else instead. Stall. If you know you are going to retreat and that this won't help the situation, then stall the retreat. If you feel that tendency to come out swinging, then stall your reaction. The spiritual saying, 'A moment of patience in a moment of anger saves you a hundred moments of regret', comes to mind here.

Let me be clear, though: stalling is not walking away. It's about hitting pause on your response.

Have you ever tried to give up something like ciggies, unhealthy food or a particular person in your life? You likely would have had to employ some type of strategy. One of the most simple is to simply create some space for yourself when the craving comes. When you crave that double-choc-coated doughnut – give it five minutes. When you crave time with that person who isn't good for you – give it five minutes. Stall your craving with time and distract yourself by doing something else.

I'm suggesting we use this concept in a slightly different way when it comes to our triggers: why don't we replace our unhealthy reactions with a pause to ponder? Our response becomes our breath.

Most yoga classes begin and/or end with the sound of 'om'. It creates focus, calms our nervous system and centres us. It's about restoring our inner peace. 'Om' is a small word with a big impact. We need to find an 'om' in our trigger moments. Instead of an 'om', let's create a 'hmmm'. Hmmm is about pondering the situation; it's about suspending judgement. It's about being and breathing rather than reacting. *Hmmm. Yep. Hmmm.* This gives us time to ponder four things:

1. What is triggering me here?

2. What is my role in this?

3. Has this happened before?

4. What is the above-the-line response?

STALLING IS NOT WALKING AWAY. IT'S ABOUT HITTING PAUSE ON YOUR RESPONSE.

Replace your reaction with wonder and contemplation. Replace something destructive with something constructive.

Now, I'm not suggesting you start 'hmmming' out loud when things go south. That would just be weird. However, what I am suggesting is that you adopt a 'posture of wonder'. Pausing for a moment can give you enough space to answer your own questions, truthfully. You'll be surprised how much this small word, and breath, can change the dynamic of a conversation. It also sets up space for a better response to the other person or the situation.

When we breathe slowly it always has a direct effect on our sympathetic and parasympathetic nervous systems. It slows down our blood pressure, sends endorphins to our brain and tells our stress reactors – our fight or flight responses – to slow. It helps us stay in the moment. So, the better we are at breathing calmly, the better we can deal with situations. But that's not the only benefit.

Breathing is proven to improve our health and wellbeing. I can attest to the difference that taking time to breathe through meditation and being more mindful has made in my life and the conversations I have every day. I react less, I own more and I'm happier as a result.

A 2015 study by psychology researchers in the US and Germany found that:

> *The emerging evidence indicates that mindfulness meditation might cause neuroplasticity in the structure and function of brain regions involved in control of attention, emotion regulation, and self-awareness.*

We now know that our brains are elastic and can change over time. That's right: they *can change* over time. Since the 1970s, clinical psychology and psychiatry has shown that being mindful significantly reduces stress and worry, anxiety, depression and addiction. That's gotta be a good thing, right? So go on, try it! You'd be crazy not to, and the people around you will thank you.

ADOPT A 'POSTURE OF WONDER'. PAUSING FOR A MOMENT CAN GIVE YOU ENOUGH SPACE TO ANSWER YOUR OWN QUESTIONS, TRUTHFULLY.

SELF-CONTROL OR SELF-EVOLVE?

Now that you are taking responsibility for your triggers, you'll be better able to recognise them as they arise and potentially before your reactions kick in. Your world will be changing; *you* will be changing. You may be realising that you have much more power in the role you play in situations that trigger you off than you initially thought.

So why have we spent so much time understanding our role and where our triggers come from? Great question. It's because managing our triggers requires both self-control *and* self-evolution.

Self-control is the ability to control yourself in situations – especially the difficult ones. It is choosing to respond in a different (better) way, even when you don't feel like it. It's avoiding falling prey to your fight, flight or freeze responses. It is overriding your negative feelings with more productive and positive responses. It shows maturity and strength.

But self-control can become tiring over time. Constantly going against our natural stress reactions requires effort. Self-control can fatigue like a muscle if we overuse it.

SELF-CONTROL CAN FATIGUE LIKE A MUSCLE IF WE OVERUSE IT.

We eventually want to get to the space where we rewire how we think, and start to view people and situations differently – in a way that serves us and them. This will mean we are no longer in a constant state of stress management. We will naturally think differently and know that how other people treat us is about them, not us. This is self-evolution.

When we rewire our thinking we may find we don't need to react to situations that used to trigger us, because the people or situations don't upset us or anger us like they did in the past. This is a sign that the triggers don't own us anymore; we are different. It means we don't need to self-control as much. To get to this space, we need to do the work on our past so we can respond differently in the future.

The way I see it is choosing when we want to do the work: is it in the moment when we are constantly self-managing and feeling stressed about things? Or quietly, in our own time? If we do the work to understand where our triggers come from, we will release the hold they have on us. This makes the future lighter and easier. We need to do the work on ourselves now, so our triggers don't own us in the future.

Is there someone in your world who used to really grate on you? Who you knew you would have to self-manage around, otherwise you might say or do something you'd regret? If you feel differently about that person now, it is probably because you have evolved in your responses and even your relationship with that person. My relationship with my ex-husband is a good one to look at here. He is a great dad – always has been. I love that about him. He had a son when I met him, and watching them together was one of the things that drew me to him. We've been split a long time now – over 12 years. We co-parent really well. As far as getting along, that's more like a rollercoaster ride no-one would pay to go on.

I describe us as oil and water: two really important elements that don't mix. Obviously, we did gel in the early days – and being together for 11 years, there were many amazing times. But it wasn't enough, in the end, to keep us together. Getting along as humans (outside of our co-parenting responsibilities) has been challenging, for both of us. I can't speak for him, as I don't really know him anymore (nor his perspective), but I can share my observations and explain my experience.

It would seem that we trigger each other. When I see his name come up on my phone, or hear him come into the house to pick up the kids, I know that I need to self-manage; I need to take a deep breath. Not so much now, but definitely in the past. For some reason, we still take what we say to each other personally. (Well, I do, anyway.) I assume he is not coming from a place of respect for me or my thinking. For example, he might make a comment about me 'being away a lot'. I mostly travel on the weeks that I don't have the kids. Client work sometimes makes that tricky, but it mostly works. We are able to be flexible with each other and work around each other's schedules, but it can be tough sometimes. When he comments on the amount of time I spend travelling, I tend to assume that he is having a dig at me not being there for the kids. I feel like he is having a crack. But that might not be true – it might not be his perspective at all.

His reactions are similar to mine when I say something that he takes the wrong way. I know my intent is good, so if I am suggesting that we could create a phone-usage boundary that is the same in both homes I do not mean it as a criticism of the way he parents. But a lot of the time, his response will be defensive of what he does at his house, and he will point out how he hasn't created this problem. That's not what I meant from my suggestion, but that's how my message has been received.

WHAT I HAVE LEARNED OVER THE YEARS IS THAT IT'S *MY* REACTION THAT I NEED TO MANAGE.

What I have learned over the years is that it's *my* reaction that I need to manage. And I mostly do. I know that how I respond to conversations or text messages is so much better than it used to be. I want our relationship to work; for the kids and for us. We deeply loved each other once, so it seems ridiculous to not get along now – especially when we have two amazing children together. I have been on a mission to work on my reactions; to understand where they come from; to interrogate what's true and what's not. And by doing that I have moved from having to actively control myself to react respectfully (well, not always) to evolving, which means I react more positively without even trying, because I am changing.

Remember, how people treat you is a measure of their character, and how you respond is a measure of yours. As you evolve, this stays true, but it is more about believing it deeply rather than recalling it to keep you from responding poorly. I still don't always react above the line every time, and this is something I will probably have to work on for the rest of my life. That makes me flawsome.

There are a lot of situations and people I would have reacted to poorly in the past who now don't trigger me as much because I no longer believe the old stories I used to about them. I still have to dip into my self-control sometimes when I'm around them, but it's needed much less often. And life is much easier because of that. Self-control is short-term; evolution is long-term.

SELF-CONTROL IS SHORT-TERM; EVOLUTION IS LONG-TERM.

Next, let's have a look at how we can start rewiring our thinking and beliefs so we can lean towards our evolution. It starts with looking at the truth.

Your cheat sheet

When we perceive a threat, we react or freeze. It's how we respond to stress. Our mind and body do not delineate whether it's a physical or psychological threat. What we need to do is to learn to look: to notice when we are responding in a way that doesn't serve us, or those around us. We can't learn or grow if we can't see what is happening.

We can notice whether our responses are helping or hindering us by categorising them as above or below the line. When we are above the line we are curious to understand, open-minded and committed to learning – even if our flaws are painful to acknowledge. We step out of denial and stop ignoring our responses, and step into growth.

When we are below the line we are closed, defensive and believe we are right. When we stay here we can become hard to be with – not just for others, but even within ourselves. As humans we fall into both categories, all the time – and that's okay. Making sure we see it is the important thing.

How we react to people and in circumstances is a choice – even when it doesn't feel that way. One way to see if we have fallen into the trap of responding poorly is to assess if we are playing the role of the victim, the rescuer or the perpetrator. Any of these roles create drama. We don't want to stay there.

We all have triggers, and unless we reach some form of enlightenment we will always have them. Knowing what your default triggers are allows you to see them before you react and to self-regulate. There are six main triggers:

1. The *content* trigger: when you disagree with the data, opinions or 'truth' presented to you.

2. The *relationship* trigger: when you are triggered by the nature of, or history you have with, another person.

3. The *identity* trigger: when your sense of self is being challenged, and your ego is wounded.

4. The *delivery* trigger: when the nature of how and where the content is being delivered is the issue.

5. The *injustice* trigger: when your sense of fairness and what is right or wrong rises to the surface.

6. The *incompetence* trigger: when you become frustrated with the lack of capability of others.

Not all triggers are bad or good; they are information to help you understand yourself more deeply. It's important to know that how people treat you is a measure of their character, but how you respond is a measure of yours.

Where do these triggers come from? Your nature (DNA) influences who you are and how you respond. We are wired to be who we are, so some things are unique to us. Our nurture (experiences in life) will influence what we believe and how we react. Good, bad and indifferent experiences will shape how we think and feel about ourselves and those around us. Understanding these is essential.

We can't always respond well in any moment, but what we can learn is to stall our response. When you think you are in danger of saying or doing something that you will regret, you can take a pause, take a breath and regroup. You do not need to (nor will you always be able to) know exactly what to do or say when you are triggered.

As we learn to see our triggers and respond better in the moment, we move from controlling our reactions to evolution. This is where our triggers become smaller and have less of an impact. It is a flawsome state.

PART III

THE TRUTH

12

WHAT'S THE REAL TRUTH?

Truth is a big concept: one we often try to make sense of. What is the truth in any situation? What's the truth when a marriage ends? Is it that you were not meant to be together, or that one wronged the other, or that someone (or both of you) fell out of love? What about when a child speaks back to a teacher? Has the child not been taught manners, or could it be that they are copying other kids? Or maybe the teacher embarrassed the child and they responded in defence? What is right or wrong, and where's the grey?

These complex issues have so many dimensions to them, yet we are quick to judge what is right and what is wrong, what is good or bad. We are quick to judge people and circumstances we know very little about. You only need to bring up a world issue – such as COVID-19, Brexit, war in the Middle East, Donald Trump or climate change – and nearly everyone has an opinion on the truth. (Often quite strong ones too.) It's game on, and that dinner party turns into a heated debate; it becomes a battle of truths.

WHEN WE ARE QUICK TO JUDGE THE TRUTH, WE SHUT DOWN OUR ABILITY TO LISTEN AND LEARN.

When we are quick to judge the truth, we shut down our ability to listen and learn; we stay below the line. I am guilty of this. I'm sure you can relate. What are you resolute about at the moment that has clouded your ability to hear others' perspectives? One of the symptoms to look out for is feeling defensive when you hear someone else's perspective. You might shut down out of frustration, or even avoid particular people, content or conversations.

We do the same when it comes to understanding ourselves. We become quite attached to how we see ourselves, our opinions and what we believe, and this shuts down our opportunity to learn.

We need others' perspectives to help us grow and evolve – otherwise we become stagnant.

YOU CAN'T FIND TRUTH IN ISOLATION

You can't find the truth unless you're prepared to look outside yourself – no matter how self-aware you are, how much work you've done on yourself or how much feedback others have given you in the past. Our understanding of ourselves and how we come across is limited if we're not prepared to listen to others. If you google 'becoming more self-aware', pick up a self-development book focused on personal growth or even engage a great counsellor, they are all likely to suggest that you ask your trusted advisers to share feedback with you about the impact you have on those around you. This way you can grow your perspective.

We can't be at one with another if we can't make peace with our whole selves. If we are living below the line we will push back on perspectives that don't align with ours, that we are not ready to hear or that we are offended by because we can't relate. This in turn makes understanding the whole truth about ourselves harder and slower.

YOUR OPINION DOESN'T COUNT THAT MUCH

Yep, you read that right. Your perspective really isn't the be-all and end-all. How you see things doesn't give you perspective – it just gives you an opinion.

The feedback you give others – whether it's about something they are doing, how they come across, their communication style or even their ideas – is not necessarily the real truth, even if you are the Dalai Lama. In fact, I love what he says about feedback: 'What you say about me says more about you, than me'. Ponder that a little. Could this be true? We often give people feedback about the things that irritate or impress us; we're affirming our biases, triggers or values when we do this.

The feedback we give others is often self-serving. This is how it goes:

► you observe something (which may be true, or not), and then

► you decide the impact (which is subjective and can change over time), and then

► you suggest what needs to change.

THE FEEDBACK WE GIVE OTHERS IS OFTEN SELF-SERVING.

This feedback process assumes that the person giving the feedback is right; it's very one-sided. See my point about self-serving?

We tend to be binary in our thinking – we see things in black and white, believing that *our* truth is *the* truth. Our opinions are deeply laid with many filters and perspectives from our nature and nurture experiences.

I love Marcus Buckingham's perspective on this. He says:

Deep down we don't think we make very many errors at all. We think we're reliable raters of others. We think we're a source of truth. We aren't. We're a source of error.

If you can detach yourself from belief systems around who is right and who is wrong, you become open – open to others' opinions; open to their truth; open to learning. This is because you are no longer wedded to your sense of what is right; you are wedded to learning, and in that space your stress responses are not even required to kick in. You have nothing to lose and everything to learn.

If this is true, then maybe the feedback you give yourself is also not the be-all and end-all, either. Maybe you need to be more open to how you see yourself and what you tell yourself.

BEING SCEPTICAL IS OKAY; BEING RIGHT IS NOT

I am a trained optimist. Martin Seligman would call it 'learned optimism' (he wrote a book all about it). My dear old mum, now passed, role-modelled it well. When I was younger, I would become frustrated by people who were overly sceptical and seemed to question everything. 'Why do you see the glass half-empty? Why are you such a doubting Thomas?', I could feel myself thinking (and often saying).

However, over the years I have learned that a bit of scepticism actually serves us well, as long as we employ it wisely. This one-liner in the book *The Fifth Agreement* got me thinking:

> *'Be sceptical' is masterful because it uses the power of doubt to discern the truth.'*

Being sceptical allows us to ask things like:

- What's true?

- What's not true?

- Is this the reality of what could or could not happen? Or is it just someone's opinion?

Listening to another person's truth or opinion doesn't mean we have to agree or take the feedback on board. It just means we need to listen and try to understand. There may be nothing correct about what the person is saying (as far as you are concerned), but refuting it without evidence and creating unhealthy disagreement isn't functional.

LISTENING TO ANOTHER PERSON'S TRUTH OR OPINION DOESN'T MEAN WE HAVE TO AGREE.

Incivility is on the rise. Researcher Christine Porath found that in 2016, 62 per cent of us experienced rudeness at work at least once per week – up from 25 per cent in 1998. With all our commitments to creating 'safe' workplaces, this is not okay.

We need to learn to have healthy conflict, where we disagree with respect. When this happens, it inspires new thinking and new ideas. Priya Parker, an expert on the 'art of gathering', tells us we should embrace a specific dispute and then 'cause good controversy that creates heat on good conditions'. What she means is we need to be explicit about giving permission to create debate and disagreement and that we can learn to do it well.

If we want to make decisions about where to live or send our kids to school, or disagree with our parents, partners or co-workers, then let's get all the negative, sceptical and challenging thoughts on the table in a respectful way and go from there. Let's be explicit about doing this and doing it well.

PERSPECTIVE IS LIMITLESS

We climb a mountain to get a better view of where we are. We try to walk in others' shoes to see things from their point of view. Gaining perspective is about gaining an **unbiased view,** so you can see things from all angles – which could include opinions that are the opposite of yours.

For years I was taught that to make decisions we need to see both sides. That's true, but it's also way too basic and binary – it serves us when it comes to conversations with one other person, but as soon as we add a third we're in trouble. If it were a formula it would look like this:

My truth + Your truth = The real truth

A while ago, one of my best mates, Hayden, made a statement that really resonated with me. He said: 'Perspective is only relevant when you have a thousand people in the room'. I've thought about that statement, a lot.

In 2017 I took my (then ungrateful) teenagers to Europe for a family holiday. It was our first overseas trip together and I had saved and planned for it for a long time. On one leg of the trip we stayed in the heart of Barcelona, in a side street off La Rambla. This was at the time when Syrians were fleeing the brutal conflict they had been experiencing for so long, and many countries, including Spain, had agreed to take in refugees. My kids, coming from their sheltered Western life, found it quite confronting to see refugees, many of them families with small children, living on the streets.

We were really torn about having an amazing trip around Europe while witnessing so many newly homeless, hopeless people suffering. I think it was the first time my kids really had their eyes opened to the perspectives of others living very different lives to their own. We were used to living among people with different backgrounds – the kids had grown up in Melbourne's St Kilda, where travellers, corporates, sex workers, addicts, those struggling with their minds and hippies all converge. Yet this situation in Barcelona felt different, maybe because we were so far from home. We wanted to help, so we decided to do what we could: we piled together the cash we had, and went to the shops to purchase some food.

I asked my son Jacko, who was 13 at the time, to go and give the food to a couple who we had passed each day as we walked to and from our hotel. He asked me, 'How do I do it? What do I say?'. I told Jacko to lean down and make eye contact with the woman, whose husband had left her guarding their post.

We knew she was unlikely to understand English, but hoped she would be able to see his intent. Jacko's sister, Holly, and I watched him walk up slowly, squat down and talk to the woman. She held his hand, locked eyes with him and they both welled up. It was an experience none of us will ever forget.

Afterwards, we talked about how different people have very different lives to us. My kids and I had seen images of the refugee crisis on TV and social media, but seeing real people in real life changed our perspective. For Jacko and Holly, refugees did not just equate to policy decisions: they were real people in devastating situations.

I'm not suggesting that my kids and I made a big difference that day; nor am I telling you this story because we think we deserve any accolades. The refugee crisis is a global issue and people seem quite set in their ways about it. The situation in Barcelona forced my kids and I to see the perspectives of many, rather than just holding on to our opinion and defending our position.

We are all entitled to our opinions, but if we hold onto them as the only truth we miss out on learning about others, the world and even ourselves. When we are closed to others' perspectives, what we hear is opposition. When we are open to others' perspectives, what we learn is wisdom.

WHEN WE ARE CLOSED TO OTHERS' PERSPECTIVES, WHAT WE HEAR IS OPPOSITION. WHEN WE ARE OPEN TO OTHERS' PERSPECTIVES, WHAT WE LEARN IS WISDOM.

When we allow ourselves to consider the perspectives of many, our formula looks more like this:

My truth + *Your truth* + *Others' truth* = *The real truth*

When we are open to collective wisdom, we move closer to the real truth.

13

WHY CAN'T WE SEE IT?

If gaining perspective and learning the truth is so good for our growth, why are we so resistant to seeking it out? The simple answer is: fear. We are scared of hearing the truth.

Fear comes in many forms. It's not just the painful, deep-in-the-gut feelings, it's the small voice that tells you, 'You are not worth it, don't speak up, you don't matter'. Fear makes us recoil from painful emotions and conflict, and avoid failure at all costs. Being conscious of our fears is important, because they get in the way of reacting in ways that serve us. Before we react, we need to be aware.

You've probably heard the phrase 'muscle memory'. It's where your body remembers, without consciously thinking about it, how to do something out of sheer repetition. In the same way as we have a physical muscle memory, we also have an 'emotional memory'. This means we have a memory of our emotional experiences and our reactions to them. If we have experienced trauma or rejection, our brains will be on high alert to these because of the pain we remember experiencing.

Being aware of your emotional memory and learning to rewrite it is important, because it's unlikely your reactions are serving you well otherwise. Managing this muscle is not easy, nor is it a once-off fix that will unravel after one glorious 'aha' moment. Bummer, right? But it's worth the effort to be aware of what your emotional memory is telling you so you can choose how you react.

IF WE HAVE EXPERIENCED TRAUMA OR REJECTION, OUR BRAINS WILL BE ON HIGH ALERT TO THESE BECAUSE OF THE PAIN WE REMEMBER EXPERIENCING.

MAKING FRIENDS WITH CONFLICT

If an outsider visited the Murch family home for a roast dinner during my childhood they would have quickly learnt it was not about the food. We would 'roast' people for entertainment. Some guests would react as though watching an entertaining sparring match between passionate communicators, but for others it was tension city.

My father loved 'havin' a good ol' Australian go' at people. In our house, conflict was a normal part of life; it was how we got our point across. Yes, sometimes we did it with a little too much verve but it's how we learned to communicate.

One of the biggest blocks we have when it comes to being with other people (whether it's our loved ones or work colleagues) is being able to listen and learn from each other. Depending on what you are used to (nurture) and how you are wired (nature), you might have a poor relationship with conflict.

Some of us are uncomfortable with it, and therefore avoid it; while others are so comfortable with it, they create way too much tension for the conflict to be productive.

There are many reasons we don't like conflict. Healthy conflict might not have been part of our upbringing or culture; we might take others' opinions personally; we could let conflict challenge our ego and sense of self; and we might have a strong desire to 'win'.

But if we are not comfortable with conflict, we will never see a change in our attitudes towards climate change, racism, child slavery or women in leadership. We will miss out on the debates that can create magic strategies, redirect relationships or help people's careers get on the right track.

IF WE ARE NOT COMFORTABLE WITH CONFLICT, WE WILL MISS OUT ON THE DEBATES THAT CAN CREATE MAGIC STRATEGIES, REDIRECT RELATIONSHIPS OR HELP PEOPLE'S CAREERS GET ON THE RIGHT TRACK.

I love Margaret Heffernan's perspective on conflict. The former CEO of five US businesses, best-selling author and popular TED speaker says, 'Conflict is good. Combat is not'. She believes we need conflict if we want to innovate and make the best decisions. However, when we turn disagreement into a 'need to win' it's no longer healthy: one party, or both, has stopped listening and is in defence or attack mode. Combat can become passive aggressive. But if we avoid conflict, we are not able to discuss the real issues. Neither of these options are helpful.

I am going to take Heffernan's statement one step further by suggesting:

Conflict is good. Combat is not. Nice goes nowhere.

Niceness can create passive agreement: where we agree with the situation so we can avoid conflict. Nice happens when we don't want to rock the boat. But it's not helpful either, because when we are nice at the expense of productive conflict we are not sharing what we really think. When we avoid conflict to make peace with other people, we start a war within ourselves. We sacrifice what we believe is important, and that's not helpful for anyone. We tend to agree with others to maintain a relationship with them, yet we compromise one very important relationship by doing so: our relationship with ourselves. By being agreeable all the time we are valuing someone external to us more than we value our internal relationship with ourselves.

WHEN WE AVOID CONFLICT TO MAKE PEACE WITH OTHER PEOPLE, WE START A WAR WITHIN OURSELVES.

Heffernan says we need to find 'thinking partners' who are not 'echo chambers' of our own thoughts. Some people think surrounding themselves with a group of people who agree with their thinking is a good thing, because they can move forward quickly and get things done. But what it actually does is stifle creativity and keep things the same.

If you turn into Andy Attacker, Robbie Retreater or Annie Awkward when conflict is at play, you are no longer focused on seeking the truth.

DO YOU FAIL OR ARE YOU A FAILURE?

I grew up in the days before mobile phones and social media. I spent a lot of my childhood outside, playing with our neighbour, Paul. In summer we played cricket; in winter it was footy (Australian Rules – yeah, not the 'real' football, I know).

Paul had an amazing collection of 50 cent pieces, which he kept in a big jar on his desk. It looked super-impressive – especially to someone who did not receive pocket money.

One morning I heard my mum shout my name in her grim reaper voice (remember that one?). She was in the laundry, going through the washing basket when she found a handful of 50 cent coins in my jeans pocket. She held them up and gave me her best 'I know what's going on here' face. (Geez I was scared of that face. You couldn't hide from it.) I was busted. Of course, you don't admit that straight away when you are nine years old, so I told her I had found them. But eventually, I had to 'fess up' and tell her I took them from Paul's jar.

When Dad came home they both sat me down. The disappointment in their eyes killed me; I would have preferred them to scream and yell than sit there calmly with their 'you've let me down' faces on. They told me I had to go to Paul's house and tell him what I had done, and return the coins. OMG, what?

I can still recall the walk of shame. It was humiliation city.

Afterwards, my dad told me he was proud of me. What the? He said he was proud that I took responsibility for what I had done; that I had the guts to tell Paul and his family, and apologise. He told me that I was strong. I was confused. Didn't I just fail to live up to everyone's expectations? Yes, my dad explained – but that didn't make me a failure. Failure is an event, not a characteristic.

We all stuff up from time to time, but that doesn't mean we are a stuff up. We need to be careful that, when we make a mistake, we don't tell ourselves we *are* a mistake. That's the difference between a mistake and shame. Being embarrassed means we made a mistake. Being a mistake is when shame creeps in. It becomes our identity; how we view ourselves.

WE NEED TO BE CAREFUL THAT, WHEN WE MAKE A MISTAKE, WE DON'T TELL OURSELVES WE *ARE* A MISTAKE.

I love how the author of *The Invitation*, named as Oriah Mountain Dreamer, talks about failure:

> *When we cannot live with failure, we limit the intimacy in our lives… [We need to talk about failure] with ruthless honesty and gentle acceptance.*

The Invitation is a book that offers us the chance to dream differently. How we view failure either becomes a shutdown or an open invitation; it makes failure a normal part of our development and understanding.

The thing is, we are more experienced at failing than winning. There is only one person in the school who gets the top marks, and only one person who wins the race. Most of us have had relationships that failed. If life were just a competition to be the best, there would be a whole lot of losers around.

When we lose or make mistakes, it makes us human. Being open to failure is helpful; creating a truth that is driven by shame will not serve us.

THE 'BOARD OF DIRECTORS' THAT LIVE IN YOUR HEAD

We all struggle with the voices in our heads, the quiet whispers that keep us feeling worthless, useless, unhelpful, not good enough, not valued and all of the other below-the-line feelings.

In 1972, American psychiatrist Dr Aaron Beck coined the phrase 'cognitive distortions'. He helped us understand that we often skew how we see things based on our nature and nurture; that these generate dysfunctional beliefs and create flawed thinking about ourselves and the world around us. The mind is very powerful, and it can convince us of something that isn't necessarily true. We can become our own cognitive hazards.

WE DO NOT SEE THINGS AS THEY ARE, WE SEE THINGS AS WE ARE. – ANAÏS NIN

Beck went on to develop cognitive behavioural therapy (CBT) – a psychological tool that has helped millions across the globe identify their unhelpful thoughts and reframe them in a way that serves them and those around them. There are up to 52 identified unhelpful thinking patterns, which is way too many to keep in mind – so I worked with a behavioural psychologist to identify the most common ones that get in the way of us seeing and hearing information that can help us grow. I call them the Board of Directors that live in our head. Our Directors are the reason we all see situations and other people from very different perspectives. Let's look at the main Directors that get in the way of us understanding the real truth.

The Always Righty

Always Righties are on a mission to prove that everything they say and do is correct. Their favourite phrases include, 'I'm just speaking the truth', 'I'm just being honest' and 'I'm not arguing, I'm explaining why I'm correct'.

Always Righties need to 'win' every conversation, regardless of the cost – even if that means hurting people they love. Apologies feel hard for Always Righties; they don't feel apologies are necessary or warranted. In extreme cases they are stubborn, combative, disruptive, arrogant, self-centred and rude. Their relationship to control is strong. They can be challenging to think with, work with and be in relationships with.

Always Righties are not good listeners, because they are busy thinking of the next thing to say to build their case. They are not searching for the truth in discussions, because they believe their opinion is the only one that counts. Or they may fall into the trap of confabulation: saying something that is fabricated or distorted, but believing it to be true (a lie told honestly).

ALWAYS RIGHTIES ARE NOT SEARCHING FOR THE TRUTH IN DISCUSSIONS, BECAUSE THEY BELIEVE THEIR OPINION IS THE ONLY ONE THAT COUNTS.

Being a strong Always Righty is often a fast track to a life of professional and personal isolation. This way of living prevents you from seeing the truth by stifling creativity and innovation, and shutting out others' opinions and ideas.

The Always Righty lived in my head for a long time before I spotted it. Searching for other perspectives has not only taught me so much but it makes me easier for others to be with. I have learned that holding on to my position or defending my opinion is tiring – for me and others.

The All about Me-er

All about Me-ers have an excessive concern for self, their reputation and how others perceive them. They believe (consciously or not) that everything is all about them. If someone does not respond to a text or email, they take it personally. All about Me-ers tend to magnify their part in other people's lives and circumstances, in both positive and negative ways. All of this prevents them from seeing the truth.

The All about Me-er's emotional challenges are often rooted in pride and arrogance, or shame and insecurity. They take everything very personally, and believe the truth is all about them. It's hard for them to see another's perspective let alone take it on board.

In *The Four Agreements,* Don Miguel Ruiz says:

When you take things personally, then you feel offended, and your reaction is to defend your beliefs and create conflict. You make something big out of something so little, because you have the need to be right and make everyone else wrong.

When we make situations and conversations all about ourselves, we can no longer see the real truth. It's all about our perspective, which is flawed – not flawsome.

The Perfectionist

Comparing yourself to others, or to yourself, can become the norm for perfectionists. There's always a sense that you're never quite enough – whether it's at work, in your relationships or in your parenting. I love what Brené Brown has to say on this topic:

Perfectionism is a self-destructive and addictive belief system that fuels this primary thought: If I look perfect, and do everything perfectly, I can avoid or minimize the painful feelings of shame, judgment, and blame.

Social psychologist Thomas Curran tells us that perfectionism is rising at alarming rates and it is causing many psychological difficulties, including depression, anxiety, eating disorders and isolation to name a few.

How many times have you been asked 'What's your biggest weakness?' in a job interview? Who will 'fess up to using the 'I'm a perfectionist!' answer? Even though we know perfectionism holds us back we are still quite happy to wear it as a badge of honour, like a signature of worth. Such irony, right?

The thing is, excellence does not demand perfection – just commitment. Commitment does not demand perfection – just showing up. The thing about excellence is that it is subjective, and often externally focused. We think we are only excellent when we win a medal, get a promotion, someone tells us we are, or we compare ourselves to others and appear to be better and stronger.

EXCELLENCE DOES NOT DEMAND PERFECTION – JUST COMMITMENT. COMMITMENT DOES NOT DEMAND PERFECTION – JUST SHOWING UP.

Perfection is a dangerous obsession. The Perfectionist living in our head tells us that we need to hide our imperfect, flawsome selves in order to be acceptable. The pursuit of unattainable perfection is never-ending because we just find a new thing to be dissatisfied with when (if) we do achieve our goals. That's because we realise once we achieve our goal it doesn't create the sense of worth that we were hoping it would.

If we're listening to the Perfectionist, it will really hurt when we receive feedback that we are not perfect. It will trigger us and spark a strong reaction. We want to run and hide from the message because it hurts our sense of self. Perfectionism prevents us from hearing the real truth.

The Binary Thinker

Binary Thinkers think and talk in absolutes and extremes: it's black or white, great or awful, success or disaster, always or never. There is very little middle ground. They don't naturally entertain the grey or naturally sit in it. If they don't do something really well they consider it to be a total failure. Binary thinking is the failure to bring both negative and positive qualities of themselves and others into a realistic whole.

When I first started my business I wanted to work with those 'great places to work': organisations that really valued their people and made their culture a priority. That led me to tech organisations. The tech industry is well known for having a strong focus on developing people, and my team and I developed a strong reputation in the industry as a result.

A couple of years ago we hired a new staff member, Jen, to help us focus on how we market and develop our client relationships. Jen kept pushing me to work with other markets and clients outside of the tech industry. I was adamant that staying in our niche was right for us. In this case I wasn't wrong, but I wasn't right either.

Jen kept pushing me to open my mind to different markets and suggested we run an 'experiment'. So we ran morning teas for those clients we didn't know to share our knowledge and experiences and see if they wanted to play. Whoa! What do you know? It worked. We are now working with some very diverse industries and types of clients to help them grow and improve.

If I'd stayed in my black-and-white thinking, which was 'We want to stay where we are and build a stronger presence', we would not have the variety of clients and services we provide today. Pushing me, when I am set in my thinking, can be a challenge; yet I know that staying stuck in one way of doing things is limiting.

We have binary thoughts at work and in our personal lives. We might decide that a particular partner is right for us or have specific views on how to parent our kids, governmental policy decisions, how we vote and how we view other people's choices. We become binary when we are right or wrong and see nothing in between.

Life is not binary, so why do we think in this way? It cripples us and our opportunity to learn.

The Labeller

Labellers make quick judgements with very little information or thought. It is easy to fall into the trap of deciding someone has a certain character flaw before you even get to know them; or predicting a particular outcome before you've had a chance to analyse a situation. How many times have you labelled an acquaintance 'aggressive' because you heard them raise their voice one time? Or labelled a co-worker 'disorganised' because they were late to a meeting a couple of times?

Labelling happens fast and easily, and we can even do it to ourselves: we try something once or twice and decide we are not good at it; we make a mistake and label ourselves a failure;

we experience a couple of relationship breakdowns and decide we are not good at love. This is where the real damage happens: we've characterised ourselves as something, so our brains then look for data to prove that assumption.

Labels can be difficult to remove. Each time you make a decision about yourself or others you are programming the way your brain works.

EACH TIME YOU MAKE A DECISION ABOUT YOURSELF OR OTHERS YOU ARE PROGRAMMING THE WAY YOUR BRAIN WORKS.

Finding your own 'truth' comes easily and quickly to a Labeller, yet we rarely hold space for other perspectives or opinions. You may have even made assumptions about this book when you began reading it. Has it met your expectations, or not?

Labelling yourself, when it's below the line, keeps you flawed – not flawsome.

The Comparer

Comparers judge things in relation to others. Their life, decisions and sense of self are not defined by their own values or goals, but by what everyone else is doing. When we process information, it is very easy for us to decide whether it's good or bad compared to something or someone else. We compare our situation to where we think we should be based on our age, our experience, our role, our peers, our friends or even where we sit in the family. We should be fitter, smarter, less critical, more critical, more confident, less confident, more sensitive, less sensitive. You get the gist.

WE COMPARE OUR SITUATION TO WHERE WE THINK WE SHOULD BE BASED ON OUR AGE, OUR EXPERIENCE, OUR ROLE, OUR PEERS, OUR FRIENDS OR EVEN WHERE WE SIT IN THE FAMILY.

We are all familiar with Theodore Roosevelt's assertion that 'Comparison is the thief of joy'. Roosevelt was the youngest president of the United States at age 42, and ranked as one of the best. His life and presidency were not without tragedy and challenges: he suffered debilitating asthma as a child; he lost his wife and mother in close succession; he fought in the Spanish–American war and was awarded the Medal of Honor for his bravery.

During his presidency in the early 1900s he made many bold changes. He was instrumental in conserving the nation's natural resources, and regulated railroads, pure foods and drugs. He expanded the Navy to show the power of the US around the globe. He attacked big business to create a welfare state and supported labour unions. He brokered the end of the Russo-Japanese war, which won him the Nobel Peace Prize. Post-presidency he led a two-year expedition to the Amazon Basin where he nearly lost his life to tropical disease.

Roosevelt knew how to push against the grain and keep moving forward, so it's fair to assume that he learned how unhelpful comparison is. Comparison kills us when we are not grounded in who we are, our own humanity and our flawsomeness.

When we feel we are not enough, we compare. Our sense of self becomes dependent on being like others. We are literally giving our sense of self over to be defined by external things and people. Others become the benchmark of our own success and happiness.

WE ARE LITERALLY GIVING OUR SENSE OF SELF OVER TO BE DEFINED BY EXTERNAL THINGS AND PEOPLE.

During my interviews for this book, interviewees often talked about a sense of shame or guilt when they experienced depression or anxiety. They said they shouldn't feel the way they did because 'others have it worse'. They told themselves they should be able to get over it. In this way, comparison keeps you in a below-the-line state; it prevents you from accepting your whole self in all your flawsome imperfection. Comparison stops you from seeing and accepting the truth about yourself and those around you.

14

WHAT DO WE MAKE IT MEAN?

Our thinking comes with its own distorted lens. As we have learned, our nature and nurture experiences dictate whether or not we are able to hold the space for other perspectives. They also contribute to what we make the truth mean.

OUR NATURE AND NURTURE EXPERIENCES DICTATE WHETHER OR NOT WE ARE ABLE TO HOLD THE SPACE FOR OTHER PERSPECTIVES.

Jacko, my 17-year-old, and I were out driving when he said to me, 'Mum, I think I've worked out life'. He said, 'It's all about your feelings. Your feelings are just made up. And whatever you decide to believe will become how you feel about it. I think it's one of the reasons why I don't let things phase me. I can psych myself in or out of things. I can decide that these Year 12 exam results are going to affect me for the rest of my life. Or not'.

Then he paused and added, 'Or maybe I am just being lazy in life and living in denial?'.

I was silent. 'Mum, why aren't you saying anything?' I responded with, 'Jacko, it takes some people a really long time to work that out. Some people never do. I'm just sitting here being really impressed'.

In their book *The Fifth Agreement*, Don Jose Ruiz, Don Miguel Ruiz and Janet Mills remind us that the greatest gift we can give ourselves is the freedom to be who we really are. It's the freedom to live without bias, disappointment, mistrust, blame or resentment. We all have the chance to choose what we make the truth mean. Often we make up our truth based on where we are at, and what our experiences have been.

So the question is: what situations are you giving meaning to right now that you might be able to change? Can you work to change your own thoughts or perspective rather than expecting the situation or other person to change? If my 17-year-old can do it, I reckon we are all in with a chance.

Now, let's look at a couple of the main ways our flawed thinking gets in the way of our meaning-making skills.

OUR ASSUMPTIONS GET IN THE WAY

We all make assumptions. There were probably times in the last week that you've become an expert in what another person was thinking or feeling. We all assume we know what is going on; it's a game we all play.

My dad has a certain facial expression he makes when he's disappointed in me. When I was younger, the look would often accompany words like: 'Well, if that's what you think', or, 'I'm sure you tried your best'. As an adult, if someone gave me a similar look, I would assume they were either disappointed in me or disagreed with me – so I would react by retreating or defending.

A few years ago, I was telling my dad about a road rage incident I had experienced when he gave me 'the look'. I immediately cried out, 'Why do you have to be so judgey? I was just telling a story!'. Dad pulled 'the look' again. I said to him, 'Dad, why are you so disappointed with me?'. He told me he wasn't, and had no idea why I was reacting in this way. I showed him the face he had been pulling. He replied, 'Darling, I don't get to see that face. I wasn't even aware I was making it. I was just listening to you'.

Wow. For years I had been assuming my dad was disappointed in me; I assumed 'the look' was full of judgement. I took that belief with me and even made it mean the same for others in my life. My assumption had not served me well; in fact, it held me back from figuring out the real meaning behind people's expressions in countless different situations.

Assumptions can be subtle or obvious. They can sound like:

'I know what he's thinking.'

'The problem with her is she believes…'

'He reckons he is better than everybody else.'

'She has no idea what's going on.'

'He doesn't respect me.'

'She has an attitude problem.'

Do any of these statements sound familiar? If someone cancels on you, do you make it mean something other than the fact they cancelled? Do you assume the person doesn't want to spend time with you, or that they have found a better option? If someone tells you that what you said was mean, do you take that feedback on board – or do you assume they are being too sensitive, or that they are naive and have no idea?

It's like you have become an amateur psychologist and are an expert in what others are thinking or feeling. It's so funny that we often can't even work ourselves out, but feel we are qualified to understand another person.

It's usually these assumptions that fuel our triggers, too – then we stop listening because we are busy being triggered off. We can't find the real truth when we are living in assumptions.

EXPECT-EFFING-TATIONS

When Stephen Hawking was 21 years old he was told he had between 6 and 24 months to live. He was diagnosed with an early onset form of motor neurone disease. His perspective of life changed dramatically. He said: 'After my expectations had been reduced to zero, every new day became a bonus, and I began to appreciate everything I did have. While there's life, there is hope'.

He went on to do remarkable, ground-breaking and life-changing work in physics and cosmology that shaped how we view the world. He died at 76 after living with the disease for over 50 years. Imagine if he had decided to sign off and just live out his final months in rest. Would we have made those advances in the theory of general relativity, thermodynamics and quantum physics? Would he have become a husband, a father, a grandfather, an author or a friend to so many?

Expectations can work for us, or against us. Hawking made them work for him, but the rest of us tend to create expectations that don't serve us.

When interviewing for this book I asked my interviewees, 'What gets in the way of you giving yourself permission to be human?' This is what came up:

- ► 'Others will judge me.'

- ► 'I will let others down.'

- ► 'People need me not to fail.'

- ► 'Fear of not succeeding; of being a failure.'

- ► 'Not meeting the expectations I set for myself and the ones others have of me.'

Expectations are the cancer of our identity. They keep us from being flawsome, from understanding who we are. They throw us into judgement, where we act according to who we are 'supposed to' be, and how we are 'supposed to' perform.

EXPECTATIONS ARE THE CANCER OF OUR IDENTITY.

Expect-effing-tations cause us to 'should' all over ourselves. Remember, we talked about this in chapter 5? Do any of these phrases sound familiar?

- ► 'I should have done better.'

- ► 'I should have seen this coming.'

- ► 'I should have thought it through and anticipated it.'

- ► 'I shouldn't have reacted that way.'

In my research, 'shoulds' were the number-one reason why people didn't give themselves permission to be human. 'Shoulds' can include ones we create for ourselves, and ones we assume others put on us. So many of us are spending so much time worrying about how we should be, based on expectations that we *think* others have of us. We worry we are not living up to others' expectations, not pleasing them or not being impressive enough. Most of these expectations have been made up; we have assumed them.

In her book *The Brave Art of Motherhood,* Rachel Marie Martin puts it beautifully:

> *Sometimes you have to let go of the picture of what you thought it would be like and learn to find joy in the story you are actually living.*

Well, I'm done with expectations! I've got some 'good enough' to meet with, some 'flawsome' to hang out with, coupled with some 'surrender to the outcomes', finished off with some 'learning from the experience'.

15
HOW CAN WE MAKE
IT USEFUL?

Emotional maturity requires us to be able to look at the truth from all perspectives; to be okay with ideas and perspectives that are not our own. This is a space where we can learn, grow and reduce our reactions and increase our knowledge. After all, a flawed perspective is like a flat tyre: you can't get very far. So how do we do that?

LEARN TO 'HOLD THE SPACE'

Ever had a blue (that's Aussie for an argument) with someone close to you who insists on discussing the issue with you right away, while you need some time to decompress before talking it through? This is a common scenario, where one party is geared up for a fight while the other wants to go into flight and take time to work things out.

I propose that time is not our solution in situations where we're angry with those we love. I reckon we need to create space to hold the thinking. We need to suspend judgement; consider another perspective; find the real truth.

'Holding space' is the conscious act of being present, open and allowing for someone else's emotional state, while simultaneously being present to your own. Think of it this way: when you hold space, you are creating a container for the other person's emotions to go into; to be seen without the interference of yours getting in the way. We can do this in a conversation. We don't always need to walk away. It's a mindset shift.

We are in a time when every gap is filled. We don't sit on a train and just think and be with our own feelings anymore; we check our social media feeds, write some texts or listen to music or a podcast. We don't just lay on the couch and close our eyes; we turn on Netflix, we devour our phones, we make lists. We don't know how to connect to ourselves and just *be*. We have, consciously or not, developed the art of *not* feeling. This means that when we do connect with uncomfortable emotions, they can be loud and overwhelming. We are not practised at holding space – with others or ourselves.

WE ARE IN A TIME WHERE EVERY GAP IS FILLED. WE ARE NOT PRACTISED AT HOLDING SPACE.

I've learned a lot about this from yoga. To hold space in your practice is to learn the art of observation; to witness 'what is'. The aim in yoga is to focus on being in the moment, rather than thinking of the outcome; to know that you will probably fall out of certain poses, and not judge yourself for it. It's also about avoiding congratulating yourself or wanting others to see if you're able to hold a pose for a long time. One of my favourite yoga teachers, Monique, talks about the power of staying in a pose until the pain dissolves. She says that in order for our bodies to evolve into a stretch, we need to sit in discomfort until our muscles stretch into the pose. It's then that they evolve.

This is the same practice we need to remember when it comes to our emotional evolution. When something that's happened to us is still painful, running from it won't fix it. Asking for time won't make it go away. However, sitting with it until it loses its power will help us evolve into a new space where the pain doesn't have the same hold over us anymore.

I am not suggesting that when we experience the intense pain of loss or trauma that we hold the space. Sometimes when pain is deep and concentrated it needs to be felt in small doses so we can survive. You can't hold a space when your heart or soul is broken. Yet to find meaning in the circumstance, over time, holding space will be a helpful tool.

So here's an idea: when something comes your way and you can feel it triggering you, the first thing is to do nothing. Yep, nada; zero; nought; zip. Don't decide whether you agree with it or not. I know this is hard. It's important to give yourself time to understand it before you decide to agree or reject it.

As we now know, we are wired to see the negatives in any feedback; our brains automatically scan for the bad bits. The problem with 'wrong spotting' is that you will always be able to find something wrong – we are clever like that – which means you are more likely to dismiss or reject the feedback before holding space for it. This means you are not able to understand the real truth.

BECOME OUTCOME AGNOSTIC

I work with lots of 'techies': programmers, developers and the like. In technology, the term 'agnostic' is quite common; a product can be 'platform agnostic' (which means it can be used with any operating system) or 'device agnostic' (which means it works on any type of device). We can create products or services that are 'interoperable' (great word, right?) with various systems – but do we apply this concept enough in our thinking? Do we come to conversations with an agnostic mindset ('I am open to the other person's perspective') or do we bring an attachment to the outcome ('I am trying to drive a decision that suits me')?

It's so easy to detect when someone is coming to you with a 'question' or 'suggestion' that is really a disguised instruction. I reckon we know in our gut when someone has their own agenda and asking for our thoughts is just a formality. It's a bit like government advertising a role so everyone has the opportunity to apply for it. (Oh, did I say that out loud?)

As we learned in chapter 9, we hear content but smell intent. I always find it amusing how people think they can disguise their intent with open questions, or a calm, eye-contact-driven nod as they are talking. But we all smell what is behind it. It's like telling a child that zucchini noodles are the same as pasta. No-one falls for that.

In the past I found it really challenging to call myself out. I've realised that attaching a preconceived idea to how I want things to go does not serve me, nor the people I am with. When we don't remain agnostic (open to one way or the other) we lose out. We lose out on learning because we are not genuinely curious about other ideas and perspectives. We lose out on building more respectful relationships because people don't feel seen or heard. We lose out on gaining real commitment because that comes when people know they have been consulted and considered.

Being 'outcome agnostic' is about ditching expectations of the outcome. It doesn't mean you don't make a decision; it's not the same as fence-sitting. It's being open-minded when you're making a decision. Walking into a meeting or discussion with an open mind doesn't mean you stay undecided; it means you remain open and curious to ideas and suggestions that are not your own. How can that be a bad thing?

Outcome agnostic is the aim. Holding the space allows you to get there.

**WHEN WE DON'T REMAIN AGNOSTIC
(OPEN TO ONE WAY OR THE OTHER)
WE LOSE OUT.**

FIND THE GOLD

As we know, one of the easiest ways to make peace with our flawsomeness is choosing to find the learning in any situation. I create the space to do so. I can make meaning from nearly anything – not because I find meaning in understanding what's going on for the other person, or why the world is behaving as it does, but because I can find the learning about how I react or how I perceive something. There is always something in there to see, to understand and to observe. I'm not suggesting we should always see every situation as positive, because some situations are just plain s**t. A broken heart is physically painful; witnessing a loved one struggle with illness or pass away is gut wrenching; being the subject of someone's poor treatment sucks. Ignoring the pain and turning it into rainbows and unicorns is living in denial. But there will always be something to learn in every situation. Focusing on what's going wrong, how crap it is and deciding there is nothing we can do traps us.

When we focus on what we are doing well and what we might do better, we grow our neural circuits and our emotional and psychological capacity. In her epic book *Mindset* and popular TED talk, Dr Carol Dweck shows that when we have a growth mindset – that is, when we think in terms of 'I win or learn' rather than 'I win or lose' – we achieve more. Similarly, researchers Buckingham and Goodall found that focusing on shortcomings or gaps does not enable learning or encourage growth – it impairs it. In the study, when students focused their attention on how they might achieve their dreams and goals, the sympathetic nervous system lit up. This nervous system is the one that stimulates the growth of new neurons which, in turn, create a sense of wellbeing, stronger immune system, better performing emotional states and openness.

If we understand the gaps and are positive about learning from them, we turn the truth into something useful.

**IF WE UNDERSTAND THE GAPS
AND ARE POSITIVE ABOUT LEARNING
FROM THEM, WE TURN THE TRUTH
INTO SOMETHING USEFUL.**

There is gold in every break-up, whether it be with friends, lovers or workplaces. There is a lesson to be learned in there for you, about you. The lesson could be that you keep trying to find your sense of self in others, or that you don't use your voice enough (or maybe too much). It could be that you let people treat you with disrespect or that your relationship with control is not good. It could be anything. The point is, it's your gold to find. Then you've got something to learn from, grow from and grow into.

DON'T CARRY A LOADED PACK

The concept of 'rucking' has been trending in the fitness space for a few years now. Rucking is exercising with a weighted pack on your back. Soldiers have been doing this for hundreds of years; only recently has it become popular with the rest of us.

Physical rucking is good for us, but what about emotional rucking? How often do we take on board more than we need to carry? Whether it's someone else's pain or stress or someone else's opinion, many of us are magnets for emotional baggage.

One of my best mates for over 30 years has just been diagnosed with Hodgkin's next to her lungs and heart. She is one of the most giving, outward-focused, generous and kind souls I know. She is not the person who deserves to or should get this. The time immediately after she called to tell me the news was really surreal. At the start of the call I had lots of questions: about the diagnosis, how she is processing it, her kids, her partner, her wedding (which was a month away). Once it all landed I started to get upset. I'd experienced this fear and sadness before, when my mum suffered from leukemia and now as my dad's health is rapidly deteriorating from many conditions. We all have stories of loss, or fear of loss, of the people we love. That's not unique. How we process it is our unique story though.

If you are a highly sensitive person (HSP) you might find it difficult to avoid taking on others' emotions as your own. I was first introduced to the concept of HSPs via Elaine Aron's books on the topic; her research suggests one in five of us process life this way. An HSP experiences life differently to others. Their senses are heightened compared to others; they process physical, social and emotional stimuli more deeply. If you're an HSP, one of the physical reactions you may experience is when your socks are irritating you because they're just not quite on right. You will connect to pain faster and more deeply so things feel worse than what you observe others around you feeling. You will be very sensitive to criticism and feedback.

IF YOU ARE A HIGHLY SENSITIVE PERSON (HSP) YOU MIGHT FIND IT DIFFICULT TO AVOID TAKING ON OTHERS' EMOTIONS AS YOUR OWN.

Whether you are an HSP or not, you can fall into the trap of carrying other people's stuff around. But you can choose not to. Jay Shetty talks about the distinction between a seed and a weed. Is the stuff you are carrying around the start of something that you can grow and learn from? Or is it a weed that will grow out of control if left unkempt? It's tricky because weeds and seeds look the same at the start, and both can trigger below-the-line reactions.

Just like we peel off layers of clothes, we get to choose which content we want to peel off or deflect from our bodies. It's up to us. Staying in blame and resentment (of yourself or others) means you are holding on to content that isn't serving you; you are rebelling and resisting it. Maybe you need to heed the advice of one of the greats and 'shake it off!' (Thanks Taylor Swift.)

This means I get to choose what pain I hold on to with my gorgeous girlfriend. I feel sad that she has to experience this sickness both physically and psychologically and go through the pain of not knowing the outcome. I can choose whether I make it about me and walk around in pain, which won't serve her or me.

I also get to choose what to take on board when others give me information about myself or others. We all need to be careful of carrying a loaded pack that doesn't teach us or grow our strength or determination in an above-the-line way.

REWRITE THE STORY

The cool thing about life is that you get to write the script for how you respond to it. It might not always feel that way, but it's true. I lost my dear mum 18 years ago. I was pregnant with my first child Jacko at the time. She had cancer for seven years before she told me and my brother, James. According to my dad, she told him that she had the sort of leukemia that you have for a long time, but that doesn't kill you. I struggled with many false beliefs when I found out Mum had held off on telling us:

► My mum and I were not as close as I thought, because she didn't tell me she had something that could kill her.

► My mum did not think I was strong enough to handle the truth.

► My mum did not want to lean on me.

► My mum was in denial that her cancer could finish her life.

Now, which one of those was true? Maybe all of them. Maybe none of them. They were all assumptions. Mum's decision to avoid telling us was her story; how I responded is mine.

I could have responded below the line with anger. I could have resented her for not trusting that I could support her. I could have become the victim. To be honest, in some moments I did respond that way.

Mum did pass away six months after she told us. We didn't know for sure if she would pull through until the last day. It was clear then that her body could not recover from the chemotherapy and the pneumonia she had developed. I got to decide how I did life with her until the last moments.

You get to decide what story you want to live out when you get news that is challenging; when you are with people who press your buttons; when you are in circumstances that are not ideal. You can even author your own narrative with 'editors' or friends around you. I love doing this; it can become the key to a life well-lived. Instead of reacting in the moment, you can ask yourself a few simple questions and reconcile them on your own or with others:

- What happened? What are the facts? (Try to detach from your *opinions* of the facts here.)

- What did I make it mean? What assumptions have I made about the other person, the circumstance or how they feel about me?

- What else could it mean? If my first reaction is below the line, what is a better way to see it above the line?

- Where is the learning? What is useful to take away about myself and my reactions?

You are the author of this journey. You are writing your own novel and the chapters are about what happens to you and the next move is all yours. You get to rewrite the middle (that you're in right now), which determines your end. If you dare.

Your cheat sheet

Sourcing the 'real truth' in any situation is complicated and it requires many perspectives. Even then, it might not be truly accurate. Just because it's true for us doesn't mean it's true in the real sense. The same goes for how we see ourselves: just because we believe something about ourselves doesn't mean it's true. We need to learn to be open; to be wrong about how we think and feel; to know that it can change and evolve. We should recognise that others' perspectives can be helpful, but we don't need to take everything others say on board.

When we walk into situations thinking we could be wrong, this can make us right. It means we are valuing curiosity over righteousness; seeking other truths rather than needing our truth to be correct. Our relationship with feedback is flawed: we tend to assume the worst about ourselves and react to negative feedback in a way that doesn't serve us, or the people around us. It's our internal negative bias that kicks in, when we let it.

When we develop a healthy relationship with conflict we are able to move through our stress reactions and decide if we need to take any feedback on board, or not.

One of the reasons we struggle to discover the real truth in any situation is that we listen to the Board of Directors that live in our head. We have cognitive biases that skew our ability to see what is true; these keep us thinking and living below the line. Some of these are:

- The *Always Righty*: when we know we are right and we are frustrated when others can't see it.

- The *All about Me-er*: when we make circumstances, reactions and anything else coming our way about us. It's rooted in pride or insecurity.

- The *Perfectionist*: it's not about being perfect but the pursuit of perfection that creates the tension. This is rooted in the expectations we have of ourselves.

- The *Binary Thinker*: when our thinking is black or white, right or wrong and entertaining grey is not a natural choice.

- The *Labeller*: when we make quick judgements based on very little information.

- The *Comparer*: when we decide if something is good or bad based on relating it to others.

The other situation that sends us into stress is when we make assumptions about what other people are thinking or feeling.

The challenge for us is how we can make all this useful. If we learn to hold the space for information coming our way, and we can see it, learn from it and avoid being offended by it, we are evolving. We can learn to became outcome agnostic, where we let go of our expectations of how someone or something should be (especially ourselves).

If we learn to find the gold in any given situation we are the ones who win. We can choose learning over reacting, and decide how much of others' emotions we take on.

We have the power to rewrite the stories we tell ourselves.

PART IV

YOUR TRANSFORMATION

16

NOW FOR YOUR TRANSFORMATION

'Transformation' is a word that tends to be thrown around flippantly. Organisations claim to be going through transformational programs; people go on retreats to transform into new people; teams go on offsites to transform into high performers. But how often are these attempts at transformation actually successful?

Transformation is not a destination; it's an evolution into infinity. It also takes time. If transformation could happen in a single weekend we'd all subscribe to those retreats. We'd fork out thousands of dollars knowing we would emerge as a new person, team or business. (In fact, many of us *do* fork out money like that, yet we don't get the results we expect.)

Transformation is a profound journey that evolves over time. Sometimes it appears as a big 'aha' moment or event, but it mostly takes shape in the small moments. The irony of it is that it's about surrendering to what is happening, and trying to understand it rather than control it.

TRANSFORMATION IS NOT A DESTINATION; IT'S AN EVOLUTION INTO INFINITY.

We can't manufacture our own evolution, it happens in its own time and it is not as illustrious or unobtainable as you may think. If you put in the work to take responsibility for your triggers, understand the real truth behind them and make them mean something that serves you, you will transform. It is that simple and that profound.

BE LIKE A BUTTERFLY

The year 2019 was significant for me. At the beginning of the year I felt like I was permanently walking through mud, and it didn't smell or taste pleasant. My gorgeous kids, Jacko and Holly, went from behaving like relatively normal teenagers (grunting, talking back, self-focused) to being next-level teenagers (getting stuck into things they shouldn't, riddled with anxiety, skipping school). They are both very different humans and I don't want to share the details (that's their story to tell if they choose), but needless to say it was tough – particularly given they split their time between me and their dad.

At the same time, I was offered the project of a lifetime. I redesigned my business around it to make sure I could take it on, but then the opportunity was withdrawn. On top of that, I received a fair bit of feedback about my style from people I respect, and was coming to terms with the fact that I had even more work to do on myself. This hurt, because it forced me to reconcile that the person I want to be is not always the one that comes across. Fark!

I experienced health challenges; hormonal changes gave me night sweats, ridiculous emotional rollercoasters and foggy brain. My dad's health was declining, fast. And to top it off many of my close friends had moved away from Melbourne. It felt like life was coming at me from all angles.

One night in particular I became quite overwhelmed. I went for a walk around my local streets. I cried it out. Crying is good: it releases hormones that can reduce your anxiety, and it slows your heart rate and your breathing. That's why we sometimes experience a mood boost at the end of a good cry. (I'm not suggesting you walk around with tears down your face whenever you need to feel better, though. That's a sign that you're not quite right. Insert awkward face.)

After my little 'mood-boosting' cry I decided the only way forward was to surrender control of everything that was happening to me. Depending on your beliefs, you might surrender to the Universe, to Mother Nature, to God or just the world in general. I decided that I didn't want to attach my feelings to a particular outcome – whether it be to do with the kids, my dad, my career or even my health. I was choosing to become outcome agnostic. (Remember, that doesn't mean you don't make any decisions; just that you ditch any expectations you have of the outcomes.)

I REALISED THAT ATTACHING A PRECONCEIVED IDEA OF HOW I WANTED (AND, IN SOME CASES, NEEDED) THINGS TO WORK OUT ENDED UP CREATING MORE STRESS FOR ME.

I realised that attaching a preconceived idea of how I wanted (and, in some cases, needed) things to work out ended up creating more stress for me – and those around me. That's because this behaviour is grounded in control: control of what the outcome should be and how I should feel about it. I wanted less of that. I wanted to focus on living life, being good enough and doing just enough without expecting things to work out in a particular way. I wanted to become agnostic about the future of my actions.

During this time, I was consistently drawn to butterflies. I saw them in my dreams, in magazines I picked up and scattered throughout my social media feeds. I even saw someone doing a keynote about the butterfly's life cycle. This prompted me to do some research; whenever I see so many coincidences in life it's often a sign that I need to look into it.

I found out that we can learn a lot from the butterfly. They start out as a genderless caterpillar where they wriggle around all fuzzy and cute. Then one day they stop eating, hang themselves upside down on a twig or leaf and spin into a silky cocoon. They become a chrysalis. And here's the really cool (and kinda gross) bit: they end up eating themselves. If you cut into one at just the right time you would see a caterpillar 'soup' mixture ooze out. This protein-rich soup starts to form the cells of the butterfly. The whole soup can start with 50 cells and finish with up to 50,000.

Once this metamorphosis is complete, he or she (now gender specific) transforms into a beautiful butterfly. The butterfly is hardwired to transform; without transformation it can't reproduce, since the caterpillar egg is laid by a butterfly. Their evolution, for survival, is imperative. Unlike butterflies, we humans are soft-wired. We can choose to transform, or not.

THE BUTTERFLY IS HARDWIRED TO TRANSFORM; WITHOUT TRANSFORMATION IT CAN'T REPRODUCE.

For me, 2019 felt like the butterfly's journey. At the start of the year I felt like everything I knew to be true was changing, and I was walking around in a haze. I felt like I was eating myself. I had become trapped in trying to control my life and the things around me so that I could feel better. But the problem was, while I could control myself and my reactions, I couldn't control my kids, my family, my team, my health or my career. I could influence them, but that's all.

The beauty of living through times in your life when things feel overwhelming is that you are just on the other side of transformation. When you surrender, you can transform and 'eat' your old beliefs that don't serve you. You become more beautiful; you can fly. But you need to trust the process.

The concept of transformation of self is not unique to the butterfly. In Buddhism, reaching 'enlightenment' is a form of transformation. The ultimate state is nirvana. Nirvana is when you end suffering, of self and others. In Christianity, we can be 'born again' into a renewed mind and spirit. Eckhart Tolle describes enlightenment as 'an egoless state'. He says it is not something you can plan to achieve in the future; you must look at your present state.

WHEN OUR TRANSFORMATION IS INTERRUPTED

If you interrupt the formation of a chrysalis, a butterfly will never form. Yet, if our evolution is interrupted it doesn't mean we don't transform. In fact, that very 'interruption' could be part of our evolution. We just don't know it yet.

We can subconsciously interrupt our own transformation by being too busy, endlessly scrolling social media, drinking, taking drugs or working beyond our given capacity. If we blame someone else for the pain or frustration we are feeling, we are hijacking our own evolution. It pays to remember the stories we tell ourselves: 'If I don't do this then no-one else will'; 'If she hadn't broken my heart then I wouldn't be in this place'; 'If they did their part I wouldn't need to work all these hours'. Any of these sound familiar?

Sometimes we can defend the very beliefs that are eating us alive. We get stuck in our old ways and are not prepared to stop controlling and start surrendering. Surrendering the outcome and owning our reactions and our roles in situations can bring us great freedom; but this requires faith. We need to believe in things unseen; that the Universe or some other higher power has our back, or that things will be okay. We need to believe that we can ride the wave.

SOMETIMES WE CAN DEFEND THE VERY BELIEFS THAT ARE EATING US ALIVE.

The cool thing is that transformation doesn't have to be big. It's happening in the day-to-day moments. As you find new learnings, your evolution is moving forward. You are being flawsome.

17

IT'S AN INSIDE JOB

Wouldn't it be great if we could outsource our evolution to someone else? We could do a contra deal: I'll look after your kids if you go and do *my* work – my emotional work, I mean. (Actually, I think I'd rather do the emotional work than look after someone else's kids; I reckon it's because I'm no longer afraid of the emotional work.) Yes, the emotional work is tough and it can be super-daunting when you're at the beginning of your transformation. But trust me: there is always a reward on the other side when you take responsibility for your 'stuff' and push through the discomfort.

YOU HAVE A RIPPLE EFFECT

A few years ago, I had an 'altercation' with my daughter, Holly, who was 13 at the time. She'd probably call it 'My mother losing her s**t'. In my defence, I was pretty tired at the time so my tolerance levels were low. I was in the car about to drive Holly to her hip-hop class, but she was refusing to get in before

I removed all the items from the passenger seat. Seriously? I breathed deeply, and made a light comment about 'her royal highness' being blessed with two beautiful hands that help her lift and hold things. I thought it was funny; she obviously didn't. She then proceeded to tell me that her dad (my ex-husband) always made sure there was nothing on the seat when she got in the car. Yep, she pulled the dad card.

Then we had a stand-off: she was refusing to get in the car, and I was refusing to move the item from the front seat. So I did what any caring, compassionate, non-petty mum would do: I reversed out of the driveway and left Holly to contemplate how she was going to make it to hip-hop.

As I drove around the block (doing my block), I calmed myself down and had a chat with myself. I remembered a principle I had learned from Jeff Olson's book *The Slight Edge*: every decision I make will push me forward in life, or back; towards success or failure. Making decisions one way or the other can be easy to do, or easy not to do. It would be easy to return home, it would be easy to say nothing, it would be easy to drive Holly to hip-hop, it would be easy to go and do my own thing. Yet, it would be easy not to as well.

However, this was not just about me. I recognised that my decision had a ripple effect on those around me. In this case it was Holly. If I did not deal with my frustration in a healthy way, Holly would also be affected. My actions could enable Holly to create a false belief that no-one is there for her. My frustration could also cause me to be short with Jacko and push him away. I could dump on my work colleagues. I could ignore a phone call from a friend because I'm too annoyed to answer, when he or she needed me. Or, depending on my decisions, none of that could happen.

The point is that the decisions I make have a ripple effect. I need to take responsibility for the role I play and whether I act above the line or below it. It's okay that we get frustrated; even that we get angry. But it's not okay to dump that on others.

IT'S OKAY THAT WE GET FRUSTRATED; EVEN THAT WE GET ANGRY. BUT IT'S NOT OKAY TO DUMP THAT ON OTHERS.

So on this particular day, I ended up driving back home. When I pulled into the driveway, Holly was still standing there, with arms crossed and disappointment written all over her face. I wound the passenger window down, leant over and apologised. I said I was sorry for how I reacted; that it wasn't cool. She did the same. I could have created a below-the-line domino effect that I could never take back if I hadn't taken responsibility for my power in this situation.

Oh, and the item on the passenger seat that I needed to remove? It was a letter. Yep, all this for a letter. Insert eye roll.

WILL YOU ACCEPT?

Acceptance – particularly self-acceptance – is hard. But if you want to be flawsome, it's essential to accept all parts of yourself so you can either make peace with them, or work on them. If you don't accept yourself, you will be in a constant struggle between denial and resistance: denying that certain characteristics are part of who you are, or pushing the difficult parts of yourself away rather than trying to understand them.

In his book *The War of Art* (highly recommended reading), Steven Pressfield describes resistance like this:

Resistance cannot be seen, touched, heard, or smelled. But it can be felt. We experience it as an energy field radiating from a work-in-potential. It's a repelling force. It's negative. Its aim is to shove us away, distract us, prevent us from doing our work. Resistance is always lying and always full of shit.

Resistance gets in the way of our evolution. It blocks us from creating peace within ourselves, getting that project done, finishing that book (yep, I know it), repairing that relationship and owning our triggers. You can't beat a river into submission; you need to surrender to its current. Just like a river, you have a current, a rhythm, that is unique to you. It doesn't mean you will always be that way, but the sooner you recognise your rhythm and know it to be true, the easier your transformation will be.

As I am writing this book, bushfires are ravaging my country of Australia. I have been having a discussion with a relative about the reason we've seen such unprecedented damage. He doesn't believe in climate change. I wanted to understand his thinking and find out what information he based his decision on. Apparently, the newspaper told him. I asked him if he had entertained the idea that some journalists and media organisations have their own agendas and perhaps their reporting could be a little biased. He insisted that all reporters tell the truth.

I could see how he had formed this opinion, and let him know this. I then asked him if he would be up for reading a well-written, fact-driven article about climate change. He refused. I suggested that maybe I could read some of the articles he sided with and we could have a discussion about our different perspectives. But no, he wasn't interested.

This got me thinking. Why was he so dogged about not even entertaining another perspective? Whether it's climate change, who we vote for, how we bring up our kids, religion or even how to pack the dishwasher, why do we get so stuck in our view and our need to defend our position, no matter what? We all have opinions on things we don't know enough about; that's not new. But why do we refuse to budge on topics that we are passionate about?

Could it be that we are scared to consider another perspective in case we discover that our thinking is wrong, misinformed or flawed? That we would need to concede that we're wrong, and that this might challenge our sense of self? If we believe that what we stand for is who we are, or that our opinions determine our character, then being wrong could seem to be a sign that our character is flawed. If we have been comfortable thinking about an issue in a certain way and are faced with evidence that we are wrong, our ego might be too self-protected to admit it.

ACCEPTANCE IS HARD, YET THAT'S HOW WE GROW.

Is it too hard to accept that your thinking might be flawed because you are human? Acceptance is hard, yet that's how we grow. What things are you resisting in your life now? Friends, work issues, decisions, conversations? If you change your mind, what would it mean for you?

LEARN TO BE WITH *YOU*

I was in an Uber the other day when I noticed the driver was taking the long way to get me home. Grrr. I could feel my hands tensing and my jaw tightening. My body was telling me I was stressed. As soon as I feel tension in my body, I know I am resisting something.

Learning to read your own signs of stress, resistance or tension is essential. It means you can decide how to act next. I had a choice: I could leave the driver to follow his map, or ask him to go the way I reckoned was faster. But to make this decision, I first needed to be present enough to notice my body was feeling tense. I need to be with *me*.

YOU CAN'T HEAR WHEN YOU ARE ALWAYS HUSTLING.

Are you a busy person? Do you always have something to do? Does it feel like you will never get to properly rest? In the last few years I have really challenged myself about what I *have* to do and what I *choose* to do. Busy people always have something they *need* to do because no-one else can do it as well as them. Often our being busy is a result of us feeling as though we are not 'enough'. It's hard to observe our body and hear the truth when we are in this space; it's like trying to hear voices in a tsunami. You can't hear when you are always hustling.

We live in a society that places value on doing stuff, being something, achieving success. If we did everything our world told us we 'need' to, we would be exhausted. The good thing is, we get to choose. Our value to others diminishes when we can't be present; we are doing, not being. When we practise stillness, allowing ourselves to feel our emotions, that's when the magic can happen. We need to learn to just *be* with ourselves.

By the way, I ended up politely asking the Uber driver about the directions his app had suggested. He agreed that the app didn't always suggest the best way, and we both had the same idea of how to travel there faster. All that tension I allowed for no reason.

OUR VALUE TO OTHERS DIMINISHES WHEN WE CAN'T BE PRESENT; WE ARE DOING, NOT BEING.

CONNECT WITH SOMETHING OTHER THAN YOURSELF

When our life is bigger than just ourselves it becomes better. We become happier, more joyful and less selfish. Why is this important when it comes to finding your flawsome? Because learning about yourself can be hard work; connecting with others can help you feel supported and less alone while you're going through this learning.

David Brooks, political commentator for *The New York Times*, found himself in a space of deep loneliness after experiencing a marriage breakdown and rifts between himself and his friends due to his work. On reflection he came up with three lies that weren't serving him:

1. **Career success is fulfilling.** (The lie of success.) Brooks had achieved 'success', but he realised he threw himself into work to avoid the shame he felt underneath. Achieving career success became a way to hide how he really felt about himself.

2. **I can make myself happy.** (The lie of self-sufficiency.) Brooks realised that we can't do everything for ourselves; that independence isn't always something to be celebrated, especially if it creates distance between ourselves and others.

3. **I am what I have achieved.** (The lie of meritocracy.)
   Brooks concluded that our assumption that people who
   have achieved more are worth more just makes us keep
   chasing our tails. (Or the tails of others.)

When he was not reaching out to others – to connect, to artic-
ulate his loneliness and his sense of loss – Brooks felt worse. This
is probably true for many of us. My research for this book proves
it, too: nearly 75 per cent of the people I interviewed said that
when they are in a dark place they nearly always distance them-
selves from others; or they keep their company but do not reveal
their true thoughts. Most of my interviewees recognised that
this did not serve them, but the shame they felt about revealing
themselves prevented them from connecting.

Brooks says we are in a 'social and relational crisis'. I think
he's right. We are better at disconnection than connection. The
irony of social media is that it was created for us to connect, yet
it draws us inside – not outside. We post pictures of our 'happy'
lives and create unrealistic expectations for others. It is a platform
for keyboard warriors to judge, not listen. Instead of spending
time together, in person, we have become digital pen pals.

WE CAN MAKE MEANING FROM TIMES WHEN WE HURT OR SUFFER.

We can make meaning from times when we hurt or suffer. We
don't have to avoid or hide from it. Theologian Paul Tillich says,
'Suffering introduces you to yourself and reminds you that you
are not the person you thought you were'. He says that only
relationships and spiritual food will fill us up when we're suffer-
ing. Suffering is not only part of growth and learning; it forces

us to dig deep into a purpose bigger than ourselves and to do it with others.

Yes, we can be proud of our independence and our ability to get things done and not be 'needy'. But we need to be aware that we can create more suffering for ourselves if our behaviour is detrimental to our spiritual and relationship needs. We need to foster interdependence – when we realise we are capable by ourselves, but better with others. It's easier to suffer when we do it spiritually and create meaning outside of our own existence.

Show me a happy person who lives in isolation of others. Show me someone who has made a life without other humans and has joy. We are wired to connect.

WALK AWAY TO FIND YOURSELF

Winnie-the-Pooh, the fictional bear created by A.A. Milne in the early 1920s, is known to say that he always gets to where he is going by walking away from where he has been. Now that's a smart bear! What does 'walking away from where you are' mean? And how does it help?

Those who have read or watched *Into the Wild* might be picturing themselves venturing alone into the wilderness, but walking away to find yourself does not need to have such a dramatic intention. It's about walking away from things that don't serve you; that keep you below the line. It could mean walking away from people in your life who keep you gossiping, or who create tension and drama. It could mean walking away from a job or company that your values don't align with. Or it could mean walking away from beliefs, assumptions and opinions that keep you from learning.

Walking away is about surrendering to things unknown; having faith in things you can't see. It's sitting in the unknown rather than trying to control your environment or the people around you. When you walk away, you recognise that you can be more present when you no longer cling to ideals, opinions, assumptions and truths that don't serve you.

WALKING AWAY IS ABOUT SURRENDERING TO THINGS UNKNOWN; HAVING FAITH IN THINGS YOU CAN'T SEE.

To recalibrate we often need to pull back; like a slingshot, we can be more powerful the further we pull back. But if we go too far, the slingshot will snap. We need to know the difference between pulling back and escaping. They can look the same, but come from very different intents.

Einstein said, 'No problem can be solved from the same consciousness that created it'. We have to expand our minds and our hearts to be able to tackle the issues in our lives. Today's problems can't be solved by yesterday's solutions. Sometimes we need to step away from our former thinking patterns to step into ourselves. We need to give ourselves permission to be exactly as we are, for now. If we are not prepared to do this, we can remain trapped – and our flaws will be the focus, rather than acceptance.

18

PICK YOUR PAIN

According to the author of *Man's Search for Meaning*, Viktor Frankl, we can find meaning in life in three ways:

1. in close, loving relationships

2. in service to others

3. in pain.

The first two make sense. Let's explore the third one. It might seem strange to think that things that torment, distress or wound us or cause discomfort could create meaning for us. But stick with me here.

Let's look at relationships. Have you ever found yourself in friendships or even romantic relationships that don't serve you? It could be that you're always the one who ends up taking responsibility for the life admin; or you always end up being friends with people who don't appreciate you. At work, do you notice any patterns? Do you seem to always wind up with a passive aggressive boss, a job that requires lots of overtime or co-workers who talk behind your back? What about parenting? Is your child driving you to drink? Does he or she show little respect?

None of these scenarios are enjoyable. They cause pain, stress, anxiety and suffering – especially when we seem to keep repeating them. To cope with these issues we tend to go into denial about the role we play, or develop self-destructive behaviours to reduce the stress.

What if we are trying to avoid the pain of the truth? If we see repeated patterns of difficult situations occurring in our lives, couldn't it be us that is the common denominator? But instead of owning that pain, we make the situation mean something else – something that is easier for us to reconcile. These are the stories we tell ourselves about others; the assumptions we make.

WE ASK OTHERS TO CHANGE, OR SIMPLY BLAME THEM, INSTEAD OF IDENTIFYING THE BITS OF OURSELVES THAT DON'T SERVE US.

Transformation and learning are available to us in these situations, yet we give the gold away. We ask others to change, or simply blame them, instead of identifying the bits of ourselves that don't serve us.

So we have a choice: we can choose to experience the pain of staying the same, making similar mistakes time after time and staying in the same holding pattern in life. Or we can choose the pain of growth: of accepting our flaws, and knowing we can think and behave below the line. Growth is about learning and evolving. Suffering holds great power when we navigate it wisely.

LEARN TO STRUGGLE WELL

The mother of one of my best mates has been married three times. All three relationships ended painfully. Her husbands either died or cheated on her. Yet while she was experiencing grief and loss, she looked truly fabulous. She always made sure she didn't look how she felt; she dressed well, put her 'face' on and did her hair beautifully. When people told her she looked amazing, she would respond, 'I know, darling. Misery suits me'. I gotta say, I love her, and her attitude, to bits. She knew pain; she didn't avoid it or deny it. She learned how to push through it. A warrior knows a battle will be tough. A business owner knows there will be painful times. A parent knows it's not all roses. My friend's mum learned how to struggle well.

I've received the gift of a broken heart a few times now. Yep, I call it a gift. The pain of being in the wrong relationship is one thing. Learning from it is the gift. This means that the next time a relationship doesn't work out and I end up hurt I will struggle through the pain better than last time. If one relationship doesn't work, I can't go to the next one thinking it will automatically be different. I am the same person, so there is a chance that it could work out in a similar way to last time – unless I have learned from the experience.

Even those who have experienced the pain of what I call 'dirty trauma' – heartbreak so intense that it throws you to the ground and kicks you in the guts and feels like it has no end – we have choices after this experience. You can either build up your walls and go back to denial or blame, or you can work through it. You can figure out the role you played (without self-flagellation) and the learnings you can take from the experience, and come back a little stronger and wiser (and more flawsome).

I have a vivid memory of my mum teaching me how to hand-wash wool jumpers when I was about 10 years old. After the initial clean and rinse, you need to immerse the jumper in clean water and keep squeezing the wool gently until all the suds and gunk rise to the top of the water. If you don't do this, all the dirt and soap stays in the wool.

I wonder how comfortable we are doing that with our personal stuff? Do we let it rise to the surface so we can see it and remove it? Or do we do an initial clean – a quick vent to a mate, a short meditation – and then move on, not realising we're walking around with slimy bits attached because we weren't prepared to do the second and third rinse?

HE MADE FRIENDS WITH PAIN, SO IT DIDN'T HAVE A HOLD OVER HIM.

My dad used to work with Herb Elliott – a former Australian athlete and Olympic gold medal winner who set the world record in the mile run, then achieved the four-minute mile 17 times. Between 1957 and 1961 he never lost a one-mile or 1500-metre race. He was inducted into the Sport Australia Hall of Fame. One night, dad asked Herb how he maintained such resilience in his training to win so many accolades. Herb spoke of his trainer, Percy Cerutty, with such pride and respect. (Look him up, if you're interested – his story is amazing.) He said that Percy would train him hard, but also spend time talking with him about other role models such as Leonardo da Vinci and Einstein and what could be learned from leaders outside of sport. During training, Percy would often say, 'It's only pain'. Herb recalled that Percy would actually train him *to find pain;* to make pain his friend. He would look forward to tasting the bile in his throat because he knew his friend, pain, was around the corner. And when pain came, he would say 'welcome'. He made friends with it, so it didn't have a hold over him. He could work with it and not hide from it or push it away. That story never left me.

The Greeks used to say that we can 'suffer our way to wisdom'. We just need to learn to struggle well. As David Brooks puts it, 'You can be broken, or you can be broken open'. We all know people who are broken and living below the line. Their brokenness is usually triggered by something they can't see a way out of. They often become victims to their circumstances and have a sense that life is against them.

Pain left undealt with doesn't change; it just takes another form. In an episode of his podcast *Under The Skin*, Russell Brand talks with Brené Brown about the saying, 'Pain not transformed will become pain transmitted'. They discuss how if we are not aware when we are suffering, we cause others to suffer as well. We stay in blame, denial and resentment towards others and life; we become joyless; we don't listen or accept advice; we are broken.

But if you are broken open, pain becomes a gift. It gives you the opportunity to experience growth.

IF YOU ARE BROKEN OPEN, PAIN BECOMES A GIFT. IT GIVES YOU THE OPPORTUNITY TO EXPERIENCE GROWTH.

Some of the most powerful movements have been created out of pain. Rosie Batty established the Luke Batty Foundation in her son's honour after he was killed by his father. The McGrath Foundation was set up to fight breast cancer after Glenn McGrath lost his wife, Jane, to the disease. Neale Daniher, who lives with motor neurone disease, created FightMND and has raised nearly $50 million. Great things come out of loss, tragedy and suffering.

There are many stories of people who have hit rock bottom only to return as new and better versions of themselves. Charlize Theron watched her mum kill her abusive dad in self-defence when she was 15 years old. She left home to pursue a dance career; at 19 she was starving, living in a ramshackle home in LA and banks wouldn't even cash the cheque she had. She's doing much better now, hey?

Robert Downey Jr's issues with substance abuse are well known; during the late '90s he was in and out of court and was eventually jailed. After joining an addiction clinic he managed to turn his life around. He landed the lead role in *Iron Man* (love you narcissist Tony Stark) and went on to become one of the highest-paid actors in Hollywood. There's also Martha Stewart, Elton John, Winona Ryder and the list goes on. (Not to mention the many 'everyday' people who have turned their pain into success.)

Now, I'm not saying we all need to hit rock bottom to blossom into a butterfly. Every bit of pain offers opportunity. We can pick the pain we want to tackle first, and grow from there. The courage is in the struggle. When something feels hard, fear pops up its head which usually results in fight or flight. But you can't have courage without fear.

Brené Brown says that courage is born from the struggle. In her book *Rising Strong*, she says:

> *Our job is not to deny the story, but to defy the ending – to rise strong, recognize our story, and rumble with the truth until we get to a place where we think, Yes. This is what happened. This is my truth. And I will choose how this story ends.*

I love that. Our job is to rumble with the truth. That's the struggle; that requires courage – emotional and psychological.

Becoming flawsome means having the courage to see our flaws, accept them, know they might require some work. Courage is accepting feedback or trying on a different truth or perspective. Courage is owning the impact you have on others. Courage is knowing you may have caused others pain.

We can't avoid the struggle, but we can decide how we want to do it.

PAIN GROWS IN THE DARK

Think about something in your life that you have either never shared with anyone, or held onto for a long time. It could be something that happened to you, something you did that you were not proud of, a lie you told, a secret you kept for another person that needed to be aired or a belief you hold that you have not shared. It has caused you pain to hold onto it, but the fear of sharing it was so strong you stayed where you were and kept it in.

We call this shame. It's beyond being embarrassed; it's where we don't feel worthy because of this unspoken thing. It makes us feel dirty, not good enough, flawed or flat-out wrong. The thing about shame is that it hides; it stays in the dark so no-one else can see it. We think if we hide it that also means we don't have to look at it or think about it ourselves. We try to keep it there as long as we can so we can continue with our everyday lives.

**THE THING ABOUT SHAME IS
THAT IT HIDES; IT STAYS IN THE DARK
SO NO-ONE ELSE CAN SEE IT.**

If we keep things in the dark, they are still there; they haven't gone away. And because we have not aired them, talked them out or worked through what is true and not true, we don't have any perspective. We unknowingly make things bigger and stronger, giving them power over us.

Let's look at something relatively small: little white lies. It's easy to see why outright lying or deception can cause suffering, because you know in your head and heart that you're being sneaky and malicious. But what about the impact of those little ones – the ones that you might even have told with good intent, because you don't want to hurt someone?

White lies can affect your mental health because they keep you in a charade. White lies aren't just said to others; we tell them to ourselves. They're like a mask that prevents us from discussing the real issue. They can lead to our own anxiety and stress, especially if one white lie leads to another. People hear your content but smell your intent, right? So, white lies disconnect you from others, because they can sense your integrity might be a bit off but they can't prove it. They can also disconnect you from yourself. Lies can affect your sleep, and your own trust issues with others. If you can't trust yourself, how can you trust someone else?

Withholding the truth and replacing it with a false one can cause us to feel ashamed – of our own deception and the tension it creates within ourselves. Every truth we choose not to look at or listen to keeps us in the dark in some way, and makes flawsome harder to reach. We can see our white lies as flaws, rather than pain that just needs to be transformed.

Gabby Bernstein is a multiple best-selling author and speaker. Her motto is, 'Be the happiest person you know'. She says:

For the past 15 years I've been on stages in front of thousands of people sharing my truth. I've willingly spoken on behalf of un-

spoken shame, sharing stories of addiction, codependency, health conditions, infertility, mental illness, and trauma. Through these stories I've healed myself and others. Sharing my truth openly has been a catalyst for growth in the world. But an interesting thing happens when you become brave enough to tell the truth. I like to refer to it as 'You go first'. When we speak our truth, we go first so we can give others permission to recognize and share their truth.

It's safer to shine a light on our shadows than it is to hide from them.

Brené Brown's research into shame and vulnerability is worth seeking out. She has created a significant shift in how we think about shame, and what we need to lean into if we want to be strong. The antidote to shame is vulnerability.

The hard thing about living in darkness is that you sometimes can't climb your way out by yourself. You need interdependence, where you learn to struggle with others and share your vulnerability in turn. The cycle is good for everyone; it's when community, friendship and life work best. It's when everyone has permission to be flawsome and work through their stuff together.

THE PARTS OF OURSELVES WE WANT TO HIDE FROM ARE LIKELY TO BE THE PARTS THAT NEED A LIGHT SHINED ON THEM.

The parts of ourselves we want to hide from are likely to be the parts that need a light shined on them. The things we're most ashamed of can end up being the very things holding us back from giving ourselves permission to be flawsome.

BEWARE OF PARASITES

Okay, let's get our David Attenborough on for a minute. We assume animals are in charge of their bodies and minds, but that is not always the case. We assume when they are together, hanging out, that it is intentional. Again, an assumption.

There are parasites out there that not only take over the body of another, they can also control their minds. Take the sea monkey. It's a weird name considering they are not monkeys and don't actually live in the sea. They are a form of brine shrimp – a novelty in any aquarium because of their fascinating looks.

The sea monkey can be infected with a tapeworm. The tapeworm drains nutrients from the sea monkey's body and castrates it. (Nice.) It changes its colour to bright red and makes it want to swim in groups. Why? Well, for the tapeworm, invading the sea monkey is only the first step in reproduction. Only when it gets into the body of a flamingo can the tapeworm reproduce. The best chance it has of being eaten by a flamingo is by becoming red, and swimming in a visible group so the flamingo can find it easily. Once this happens, the tapeworm moves into reproduction mode to complete its life cycle. Yep, that's right: the tapeworm hijacks the sea monkey's brain and body to complete its development. (The good news is that the tapeworm can protect the sea monkey from arsenic poisoning, so it can't be all that bad, right? I'm always looking for a positive.)

Parasites are quite small and spend a lot of time in other hosts. They are easy to overlook. Parasites on their own are so small you can't see them, but they draw together quickly and become an issue. In the way that some animals do not pick up that a parasite is about to take over their mind, we too miss the cues when unhealthy thinking patterns and poor decisions take us over. It's the parasites we unknowingly let in that create unnecessary pain. We end up in a battle in our heads as we no longer know what's really true.

WATCH OUT FOR PARASITES, BECAUSE THEY ARE QUICK TO TAKE OVER AND START CONTROLLING YOU.

Any thinking that is below the line, that holds you back from seeing yourself in a flawsome way or that keeps you in fight or flight mode could be named a parasite. Watch out for parasites, because they are quick to take over and start controlling you.

19

HOLD THE SPACE FOR FLAWSOME

We spoke about holding the space for the real truth in chapter 15; how we can more easily see the truth, if we can suspend judgement of our opinions and assumptions and hold space for what's really going on. Let's take it a step further. Can you hold the space for yourself to be flawsome — to accept that you are flawed and will think and behave both below and above the line? Can you be okay with accepting the good bits as well as the things you're not so proud of? An athlete knows that most days they will wake up in pain; they create space for that. Why can't we?

CAN YOU HOLD THE SPACE FOR YOURSELF TO BE FLAWSOME — TO ACCEPT THAT YOU ARE FLAWED AND WILL THINK AND BEHAVE BOTH BELOW AND ABOVE THE LINE?

I was in Byron holidaying with a friend of mine, Charlotte. We were on our way to a gorgeous little clothes shop (Spell & the Gypsy – check it out). It was a really hot day. We walked past a mum with two small kids. The little girl, who would have been about five years old, was complaining about the heat. She was putting on her best whingey-whiny voice: 'Muuuum, it's too hot. I can't see. The sun is in my eyes'. I walked past and said, 'Yeah, you need a hat, don't you?'. A moment later I realised Charlotte was looking at me incredulously. 'Did you just Mum-shame her?' she asked. 'OMG', I replied, 'I just realised. I fully did'.

Many years ago, I might not have owned my behaviour. I might have been so embarrassed that I became defensive, saying something like 'Well, the mum should have thought about a hat for her kid before she left'. Now, my intention in this scenario was not to shame the mum; I was just trying to make conversation with her cute little girl. But I could see the implications of my comment once I'd said it. The mum responded to her kids, 'Lucky we've got sunscreen on you then!' (loud enough for me and Charlotte to hear). So, my guess (although I don't want to make assumptions ;-)) is that she felt shamed. Oh gawd. Flawsome Georgia strikes again.

Can you hold the space for the things you've said and done that you feel bad about, or the truths you've kept in the dark? Can you air out those lies, big or small? Can you admit to yourself that you are not always awesome – that you fail at stuff (but you're not a failure)? If you treat someone poorly, can you own that but realise you're not a bad person overall? Can you be brave enough to admit to yourself, and to others, that you have work to do on yourself? That you are a normal, flawed, sometimes triggered, defensive, retreating, unhelpful, sometimes selfish human? I can – not always in the moment, but at least afterwards.

I AM UN-WEDDING MYSELF TO THIS RIDICULOUS NOTION THAT I AM NOT ALLOWED TO FAIL.

I am un-wedding myself to this ridiculous notion that I am not allowed to fail. I've learned, and I am still learning, to hold the space to think about it, look at it, question it, acknowledge and own it. I know that facing up to my flaws will feel bad. I will feel guilty, even ashamed. But I will work to move through, because if I don't allow myself the time and space to acknowledge my flaws I am picking the pain of the same. I don't know about you, but I'd rather pick the pain of evolution so at least I'm being productive.

AWARENESS CREATES BREAKTHROUGHS

At some stage we need to break the automatic cycle of responding to our triggers. If we can't see our responses, we are not able to shift them. If we are not able to see our triggers in the moment we will respond as we always have – as our bodies know, and our mind is used to.

In his book *Stop Missing Your Life,* my friend Cory Muscara tells us that being human is hard. He says that if we can become more aware of what we see, feel, experience and think, then we can move forwards.

Cory is an expert in mindfulness. I've read a lot of books on the art of mindfulness and I love his description a lot:

This is not about meditation. This is about intentionally moving closer to our human experience, learning how to dance with it, to be at peace with it – maybe even enjoy it. It's not about clearing your mind. It's about developing an awareness of what is going on in our mind and being intentional about where we direct it. The day, from start to finish, is a playground for presence.

Cory teaches us that simply being courageous enough to see and notice what is going on and how we are reacting allows us to develop the internal freedom and growth that we were destined to have.

AWARENESS IS SOMETHING THAT WE CULTIVATE AND TEND. IT'S A PRACTICE THAT REQUIRES PRACTICE.

Awareness is something that we cultivate and tend. It's a practice that requires practice. We need to learn how to create the space to do this – and this can be done ourselves, without paying thousands of dollars to experts.

How we experience triggers, truths and moments will profoundly affect our responses. How we experience pain will allow us to move forward. As Cory says:

As we develop these inner resources, we simultaneously expand what is called our 'window of tolerance', the capacity of our nervous system to be in the present moment without shutting down or getting overwhelmed. When we can meet pain and discomfort without shutting down, we give our walls an opportunity to soften. And when our walls soften, we make contact with our life.

Do yourself a massive favour and read Cory's book. It shows us an amazing path to freedom and teaches how to hold the space.

CAN YOU BREATHE?

Have you ever defragged your computer? Defragmentation is a process that helps computers access files on the hard drive faster. Just like your computer, you need to create space and time to reset how you think, feel and be. Breathing helps us do this. I'm not referring to the regular breathing you are doing now; I mean the intentional, present kind of breathing that helps us relax into the present and stop focusing on the shame of the past and the anxiety of the future. In a way, breathing is about resetting our own internal files so we can see things clearly and access truths that will serve us. It enables us to search for the truth without escalating to fight or flight mode.

Breathing is powerful. It allows you to take a step back from whatever is bothering you. It expands your brain's capacity to think more clearly. In times of stress, it calms your nervous system. Breathing can be your superpower.

BREATHING CAN BE YOUR SUPERPOWER.

Right now, I want you to try this. I want you to breathe through your nose. Breathe in for three slow counts. Hold for three counts. Breathe out for three. Hold for three. Do this two more times.

What have you noticed? Did you feel your body relax just a little? Did your mind become a little less cluttered? Were you more conscious of where you were lying or sitting? Did you sit up more or relax more?

Breathing works. It helps us connect to ourselves, to hold the space for where we are at. We just need to learn to do it mindfully, to help us be in the moment.

20

GET STUCK IN GROWTH

In chapter 18 we discussed how we can choose our pain: the pain of staying the same, or the pain of growth. For me, it's a no brainer: I choose growth. I am committed to my own evolution. Will I miss opportunities to do this? Abso-friggin-lutely. I am human. I might intentionally miss growth opportunities, or it could happen subconsciously. What I want to be able to do is evolve so I no longer feel triggered when I am with myself, with others and making my way through the world. Will there be a time when I am never triggered? That's a big, fat 'No' from me. I am not prepared to do that much work. I am okay with the pace of my evolution, for now.

Controlling my reactions to respond well requires short-term control. Evolving so I am triggered less often is long term. Growth takes time, but if you're committed to it you will be surprised to find you're evolving in ways you never thought possible.

FIND YOUR INNER MEERKAT

I have a fascination with meerkats; they are so funny to watch. They are naturally very curious animals and are known as one of the most cohesive mobs in the animal kingdom. They all forage for food as a group with one or two who 'stand sentry' to keep an eye out for predators. They babysit the children whether they are the parent or not. Females will even lactate to feed babies that are not their own. If one meerkat is being attacked by a cobra, the others in the mob will form a circle around the cobra to intimidate it into retreat. Another cool thing about them is that they have an immunity to some venoms. When they are stung they either shake it off or are unwell for a few days until they recover.

I think there are a couple of lessons we humans can learn from meerkats. While they work together well and need each other to thrive, they take responsibility for the role they play in their mob. We could do that better at work and home I reckon.

They are remarkably curious about their surroundings – they're always sniffing and foraging. We could be more curious when it comes to things we can't easily see, hear or understand.

When other people sting us with their words or situations trigger us, we could remain immune. We could get curious about the other person's perspective and try and understand the real truth. Or we could choose to not carry the ruck.

I wish you could see my meerkat impersonations. They are good (self-assessed, of course). I would be standing super-tall, on my tiptoes, with my hands held like paws just under my chin. I'd be quickly darting my body and head one way, then the other. And when something comes and stings me, I would look at it and shrug my shoulders. I'd keep foraging around, moving forwards. Let's get our meerkat on when it comes to learning.

If something stings us, we have a choice: to be curious about where it came from; to be curious about our reaction.

I love Cory Muscara's simple formula to develop wisdom:

Experience (your life) + Curiosity (a gentle wondering) = wisdom

The Buddha didn't reach wisdom by thinking about being peaceful. The swimmer didn't become an athlete by watching swimming programs. Becoming flawsome is about truly knowing and understanding your life experiences and looking at them through a lens of curiosity. To do this requires patience and curiosity.

KNOW THIS: YOU WILL DISAPPOINT OTHERS

In 2019 I levelled up in my career. I was offered a leadership role in which I would be involved in helping shape an organisation and would work with people I love. I was excited. But with a new role comes expectations – from yourself and, I soon learned, from those around you. The more responsibility you have, the more people expect of you. I knew the colleagues I was working with; we had worked together before, but not to this extent and not with me in my new role.

After some time in my new role, I learned that some of my colleagues had shared some feedback about me with our CEO. It wasn't all joy, love and unicorns; there were words in there like 'dismissive', 'aggressive' and, worst of all, 'dangerous'. These words came from people I trusted, valued and respected. They hurt. I was upset that people saw me that way, and that they didn't feel comfortable or even safe with me. The worst part was that I had really been working on myself; I thought I was starting to nail the self-awareness and become much more mindful of the impact I had on others.

I went digging for examples of when and where I had made people feel this way. A couple of situations were recent, a few occurred years ago and some people had no examples at all – it was just how they felt.

So I had choices. I could:

- ► reject the feedback and deny its truth

- ► be offended and blame people who couldn't provide solid examples

- ► be pissed off that people were talking about me behind my back

- ► search for the real truth and take ownership of the role I played in others' experiences of me

- ► forgive people for talking about me, rather than to me

- ► forgive myself for treating people as I did

- ► learn from it all so next time I could see or feel myself about to do the same thing I would be able to pull back.

What did I choose? A bit of all of them, to be honest. I started in denial: 'I am not that person'. I moved to being mildly offended that people didn't come to me (although I moved on from this way of thinking quickly, because I know why people don't; I get it – I've written two books on feedback). I took responsibility for what I said and did, and came to an understanding of how others felt. I am proud I moved into forgiveness. I called those who I had wronged; I apologised and thanked them for sharing their experience. Then I did the harder one: forgiving myself.

It was a still, crisp spring night and I had just got off the phone on a call with the CEO – my friend, Pete. He told me to learn from it and move on; to forgive myself. I went home, had a shower and washed off the experience. Then I did a few blocks of my local streets and did just what Pete suggested: I forgave myself. I made peace with my humanity. I stepped into my flawsomeness.

This situation was a pivotal moment for me. It reminded me that when you think 'I've evolved' the irony of life shows you that there is no such space. I learned that I will always disappoint people; it's in my nature and nurture. I learned that I have a choice about how I respond and rewire. Once again, how people treat you is a measure of their character; how you respond is a measure of yours.

I LEARNED THAT I WILL ALWAYS DISAPPOINT PEOPLE; IT'S IN MY NATURE AND NURTURE.

I am flawsome! I'm so glad I chose not to stay in denial and numb the pain. I'm proud I went head on into learning. I decided in that moment that this was what I would do from then on. I chose the pain of growing rather than the pain of staying the same. I would rather have people tell me how they experience me or my work than not. Sure, it hurts to find out you are not a superhero; but I know I will get there if I stay open to learning.

You will let people down; whether it's via something you did or did not do; or something you had no idea would impact others. That doesn't mean you need to live in disappointment. As Dita Von Teese says, 'You can be the juiciest, ripest peach in the world and there's still going to be people who hate peaches'.

REWRITE YOUR BELIEFS

For over 15 years I have been drawn to a memory I have of my ninth birthday party. We were playing pass the parcel. Mum was making sure the parcel went around fast enough and that everyone got a hold. Dad was on the music. Mum had wrapped the parcel with a little gift inside each layer so that everyone got a present when the music stopped. It hadn't stopped on me yet.

The parcel was getting smaller and smaller. Finally, the music stopped for the last time – not on me. I can't remember what the final gift was, or what happened straight after – but the next thing I knew, I was in my bedroom with the door shut. I had been told that if I was going to act like a spoilt brat I could go to my room.

You might be thinking, 'But Georgia, it was your birthday – you had probably already received dozens of presents'. Yes, I know. But that feeling I had in my bedroom has never left me: I felt really alone.

This memory has come up so many times for me and it wasn't until last year that I understood why. I attended a healing ministry, with three ladies who are experienced in the art of helping people move through past pain. Now, I had no idea what was going to come up in that session. I thought it might help me deal with my mum and dad stuff or past lost loves or broken friendships. (Yep, I was creating expectations again rather than being outcome agnostic.)

The ladies asked what memory was coming up and I reluctantly told them about my birthday party. They helped me to relive the moment, as if I were back in my room, crying and feeling so alone. They asked me what I believed in that moment. It was then that I realised it had nothing to do with not getting a present. In that moment, I had decided two things about myself: that I am too needy, and that I will always be on my own.

Now the floodgates of shame tears were opening. We talked about the areas of my life in which these beliefs have played out in negative ways. I realised that, for most of my life, I had walked in these beliefs. I have always believed that I am the needy one in relationships, and that I will always be alone.

I GOT TO REWRITE MY BELIEFS THAT DAY. I WALK LIGHTER NOW.

I got to rewrite my beliefs that day. I walk lighter now. Most of the time, I do not believe people see me as needy (although I am still working on this). I know I am not on my own. How I live has changed. When someone in my personal life doesn't return a call or cancels a catch-up, I don't try to make that mean anything other than what it is. In the past, I would sometimes think people did that because I am too needy, but now I know this is not so.

When I get close to people, I am now less concerned about whether it will go somewhere further. Rumi was right:

Your task is not to seek love, but merely to seek and find all the barriers within yourself that you have built against it.

It now makes sense why this memory kept coming up: I needed to process it. My faulty beliefs dictated how I connected with others. Our childhood memories are strong and powerful, but our beliefs about them are often untrue. We just need to find ways to work through them and be prepared to go to the difficult places in our minds.

FORGIVENESS IS *YOUR* GROWTH PILL

When Tyra Banks was called a 'super-waddle' she had choices. She could have resented the press, taken it personally and felt rejected – both physically and emotionally. She could have gone on a media rant to criticise the critics. She could have taken the feedback on board and let it define her sense of self. After all, her career was all about looking fabulous. Yet she didn't. She rose strong.

Tyra turned the experience into an opportunity, because she is a professional. Professionals know that others will be haters, others will criticise, others will blame. They know they have a choice about what they take on board and learn from and what they dismiss. They don't make it personal. They treat criticism with compassion and forgiveness: compassion for self, forgiveness for others.

PROFESSIONALS TREAT CRITICISM WITH COMPASSION AND FORGIVENESS: COMPASSION FOR SELF, FORGIVENESS FOR OTHERS.

The thing about forgiveness is that it's not a gift for another. It's a gift for ourselves. Forgiveness helps *us* move forward, so we can stop the cycle of pain transferred from one to another.

Forgiveness is not easy. It can take time, but it should be carried out on our own terms. We need to be patient with ourselves and accept that it can be a slow process. In his book *The Mastery of Self*, Don Miguel Ruiz Jr says:

> *Respecting yourself also means being honest with yourself. If you are not ready to forgive, that is your truth. Don't subjugate*

yourself with 'I have to'. If you are not ready, you are not ready; and the acceptance of yourself with this truth is practicing unconditional love… Forgiving is the final step of healing a wound.

We just need to know that the battle in our heads will continue until we can move to a place of forgiveness. Awareness of this is key.

We are not perfect. People will tell us so, because that's their truth. We don't have to make it ours, or be offended by it. Dropping offence and stepping into compassion – forgiving others for the words or actions that triggered us – is above the line. Forgiving *ourselves* is evolution. We are often our own worst critic. We are experts in punishing ourselves.

You are likely to have to keep taking the forgiveness pill. Sometimes daily; sometimes hourly. We do life with flawsome people. We make mistakes often. It's okay. We can forgive, and be forgiven.

I constantly need to forgive myself for putting my (unwarranted and not asked for) opinions on others. I'd love others to forgive me for doing so. Luckily my friends are gracious; they know my heart. Unless of course I've pushed it too hard. My friend Annie will give me 'the face'; I have learned that I have overstepped the mark when I see this. The more I am aware of the role I play, and the more I forgive myself for it, the less I do it. Mindfulness works. Who would have thunk it?

HAVE A MEETING WITH YOURSELF AND SEE WHAT NEEDS TO BE ON YOUR FORGIVENESS AGENDA.

Have a meeting with yourself and see what needs to be on your forgiveness agenda. Percolate in it. You may not have deserved whatever you've been on the receiving end of, yet you have a choice about how you respond. You can be bigger than the experience. Your destiny is not to walk around holding grudges against others or yourself. That was never the plan.

FIND YOUR SUPERPOWER

My mate Callum McKirdy is flawsome. Callum is one of those guys who everybody loves. He's endearing, kind, funny and thoughtful. He's all about the people he is with. And, like most humans, he doesn't see himself like we see him. But that's changing.

He's in the process of making his flaws his superpowers. For his whole life, Callum has struggled with things that most of us take for granted — such as filling in forms, using ATMs, shopping online or using e-kiosks. He's a super-competent facilitator, mentor and speaker, but some other tasks were always hard. And instead of articulating that, he would hide it. He would create ways to cope with it rather than 'fess up to those around him.

It wasn't until 2019, when he was diagnosed with ADHD and dyslexia, that he realised how much energy and time he spent on trying to do 'normal' things. It wasn't the diagnosis itself that was significant; It was being able to give a name to the things that held him back. He can now see that the way he lived his life held him back and created self-limiting beliefs.

Callum says:

Let me be clear — neither dyslexia nor ADHD are disabilities; they're naturally occurring neuro-types that happen to be a minority. The western world has been established on norms defined by the majority, which is why systems are more difficult for neuro-divergent people to cope with and adapt to – education, the internet, commerce, etc. have been designed for the beer-belly of the bell-curve, not the extremes.

Callum doesn't wear his diagnosis as an excuse; it's just allowed him to understand himself. He calls himself 'ADHD positive'. I love this so much. The super-cool thing is that he has used who he is and moulded it into his superpower. He has surrendered to it and allowed himself to be flawsome. Callum says:

I've now found a niche for myself helping leaders uncover, unlock and unleash their potential – the difference and uniqueness of their collective group. I can now help others harness the power of people with different minds and ways of doing things. I've found my place using the superpowers often characterised by neuro-diverse thinkers.

He is an example of ownership without it being an excuse. He's not the guy who says, 'I can't do that because I have ADHD'. He hasn't made it his identity; it's just a way to understand himself. For the first time in his life, he says he knows who he is now. He's longer an outcast.

Who we are – our characteristics, personality, physical self and wholeness – is our superpower. The challenge is in connecting to it (not being triggered by it), surrendering to it (finding the truth in it) and letting it evolve (the transformation). We all have the opportunity to do this.

WHO WE ARE – OUR CHARACTERISTICS, PERSONALITY, PHYSICAL SELF AND WHOLENESS – IS OUR SUPERPOWER.

I have always been a little bit obsessed with female superheroes. When I was growing up I loved the Bionic Woman (Jaime Sommers) and Xena the Warrior Princess (a New Zealand icon). I also had an extra-special place in my heart for Wonder Woman. I was fascinated by her Lasso of Truth: all she needed to do was put her lasso around someone and they were compelled to tell the truth. That was her superpower.

Imagine if we had our own Lasso of Truth for ourselves. Our lasso could cut through the fears, the shame and the assumptions we make about ourselves and just get to the bottom of it. The good thing is, even without a lasso we all have the power to rewrite the truth about our supposed flaws. We can turn them into our superpowers, if we dare.

CHOOSE USEFUL BELIEFS OVER LIMITING ONES

In 2019, Jacko was doing Year 11 and also completing one Year 12 subject – Maths Methods. Towards the end of the year, he decided not to hand in his final project for Media Studies and instead put his energy into the two Maths Methods exams – since these would count towards his final school score.

I found out that he didn't hand in his final project via an email from his teacher. Jacko had decided to rely on the 'ask for forgiveness, not permission' theory. If he had subscribed to the rules of school, he would have had to hand the project in because the school said it was part of his Year 11 results (and rightly so). But Jacko decided that wasn't a good enough reason or the best use of this time.

I am not advocating rebellion here, but I am open to a good argument. Jacko is not defined by what the school thinks; he's nearly an adult and living by his own rules. The thing is, we all have access to amazing teachers, past and present, these days via the wonderful world of the internet: Gandhi, Brené Brown, Thich Nhat Hanh, Barack and Michelle Obama, Nelson Mandela, Maya Angelou, Jay Shetty and more. There are many who offer great advice about a smarter, happier, better way to do life. The cool thing is that we get to choose to listen and act on their advice, or not. That's the great thing about having a free will, right? Yet, as we lose our innocent mindset, we often fall into the trap of living by rules that don't serve us.

As kids we run around naked in the grass with the sprinklers on, we wear clothes that don't match, we say things that don't make sense, we talk to strangers like we know them. Then, as we grow into our adolescence, we become conscious of the world we live in; the world that creates 'rules' around how we should dress, eat, dance, work and hold our knife and fork. And we believe them. We believe ads on social media that our teeth are not white enough; a sexual partner says we should really be more open to exploring things so we decide we need to do that.

We choose to believe these rules so we can be enough – not just for ourselves, but for everyone else. This is where we form an image of perfection.

WE CHOOSE TO BELIEVE THESE RULES SO WE CAN BE ENOUGH – NOT JUST FOR OURSELVES, BUT FOR EVERYONE ELSE.

The authors of *The Fifth Agreement* propose that we are perfect as we are. It's our beliefs that we picked up along the way that get in the way of us believing this. We believe the saying 'No-one's perfect'. I say pffft, we are. We just don't know how to believe it yet. We are blinded by the lies we have been told about what perfection is.

Like Jacko, we can create new rules that serve our purpose better. We just need to keep in mind we have to live with the consequences and think about whether they will hurt others around us.

Oh, and Jacko, thanks for the reminder. Maybe just give me a head's up before your teacher emails me next time. ;-)

Your cheat sheet

Growing into your flawsomeness is only moments away. You won't complete your entire transformation at a far-away retreat or with a single 'aha' moment. It will happen in the everyday small revelations. It can be as simple as recognising your triggers, searching for the real truth and making it mean something that serves you: that helps you to grow and find the gold. Yet surrendering to that can be hard. It requires courage to own the parts of ourselves we are not proud of and to rewrite false beliefs. It doesn't require other people or circumstances to change; it requires us to rewire. It's an inside job.

Taking responsibility for the ripple effect that we create in the world is not just mature, it's empowering. It says: I know I am human and I will always be flawed yet I will accept the role I play and learn from it each time. I won't resist it or push it away. I will learn to be with myself in all my flawsomeness.

Vulnerability cannot be bypassed. To be honest with ourselves and with others requires courage, because sometimes it's painful.

Growth requires a choice: it's picking the pain of growth over the pain of staying the same. Neither option is easy, but one of them leads you to evolution and the other does not.

Life will always throw us curve balls that we did not ask for, nor can control. The key is learning to struggle well: to sit into the discomfort and understand it. Whether it's stuff from the past that we need to reconcile or things that happen in the future, wrestling with the truth is a game changer.

When we don't connect to the things that cause us pain or discomfort they can become bigger and overtake us. The antidote is connection – to self and others. If we can learn to be okay with the difficult moments and move through them, we are in evolution. If we can learn to be present, to be aware of what is going on, this will be enough. We often make our growth more complicated than it needs to be. Getting stuck in growth is a much better place than being stuck in our stuff. When we learn to be curious about what is going on around us and in us, we are healthy. We can question our triggers and our truths and decide what serves us and what doesn't.

Know that you will disappoint people. We are human. We are flawed. This is okay. Know that your best, in the moment, is good enough and that's all you need to ask of yourself.

If we rewrite our self-limiting beliefs we learn that our imperfections can become our superpowers. And the cool thing is, it's as close as a belief away.

THE BIG (LITTLE) FINISH

Your quest doesn't finish here. Nor did it start when you first opened this book: it's been ongoing since you were born. The next move is up to you, so ask yourself: what stories am I telling myself that no longer serve me? How am I hiding from the truth?

Remember: to be flawsome involves not just accepting your flaws, but understanding where they come from. It's not just making peace with your flaws; it's knowing that without them, you would not be you. So, don't make information the enemy: you give your power away that way. You have the power to choose whether you would rather feel the pain of staying the same, or the pain of transformation.

What is your choice? Would you rather seek the truth and work through your pain and triggers so you can gain a true understanding of yourself and your experiences? Or are you going to stay in blame, denial, resentment and mistrust?

Transformation lies in the courage to choose discomfort and take responsibility for yourself and the impact you may have on those around you. If you choose flawsome, you can do this without needing to take shame on board.

TRANSFORMATION LIES IN THE COURAGE TO CHOOSE DISCOMFORT AND TAKE RESPONSIBILITY FOR YOURSELF AND THE IMPACT YOU MAY HAVE ON THOSE AROUND YOU.

It's as simple as noticing your triggers. See them. Name them. Take responsibility for them. They are yours. Seek the truth. Be open to many perspectives. Don't take differing ideas, people or situations personally.

The simplicity of it all is that transformation comes from inside. It's not a place you need to go to. It's just a matter of finding the gold.

To finish, I will leave you with one of the most beautiful statements by Elisabeth Kübler-Ross. Elisabeth was a Swiss-American psychiatrist, recognised in *Time* magazine as one of the '100 Most Important Thinkers' of the 20th century. She is well known for her expertise in grief, which led to development of the Kübler-Ross grief model. It's been used globally for nearly 40 years. Elisabeth said:

> *The most beautiful people we have known are those who have known defeat, known suffering, known struggle, known loss, and have found their way out of the depths. These persons have an appreciation, a sensitivity, and an understanding of life that fills them with compassion, gentleness and deep loving concern.*

Elisabeth understood that pain needs to be moved through; that it's a process. If we don't allow the process to unfold and deal with what arises, we can become stuck. When we don't recognise and own our triggers, we become stuck. We pick the pain of staying the same.

WHEN WE DON'T RECOGNISE AND OWN OUR TRIGGERS, WE BECOME STUCK. WE PICK THE PAIN OF STAYING THE SAME.

We will always oscillate above and below the line in our thinking and behaviours. This is what makes us human. To be flawsome is to know this. But we don't use it as an excuse to stay the same. Flawsome people are inspired to grow to be the best version of themselves, yet they know that who they are is okay too. They're full of flaws and awesome because of them.

There is no need to be perfect to inspire yourself or others. Let the people around you be inspired by how you deal with your imperfections. Let flawsome be your superpower.

LET THE PEOPLE AROUND YOU BE INSPIRED BY HOW YOU DEAL WITH YOUR IMPERFECTIONS. LET FLAWSOME BE YOUR SUPERPOWER.

My hope for you is that you are able to learn from this book; that you become committed to your evolution, while knowing you have flaws and there will always be work to do. I hope you can know that this is enough.

You have the power to be flawsome, just as you are. You just need to choose to accept this.

WHAT YOU COULD DO FOR ME

A big, deep-hearted thank you for taking the time to read and digest my passion and my journey. If it has resonated with you, I would sincerely value your review on Amazon. I would love to get this message out to more hands and hearts, so we can all learn to do this crazy journey of life together – better, in all our flawsomeness!

Again, thank you.

Georgia

FURTHER READING

Part I: The pursuit of flawsome

Elliot Aronson, Ben Willerman and Joanne Floyd, 'The effect of a pratfall on increasing interpersonal attractiveness' *Psychonomic Science*, vol. 4, 1966.

Malcolm Gladwell, *Outliers: The Story of Success,* Back Bay Books, 2011.

Adam Galinsky and Maurice Schweitzer, 'The Secret to Getting Other People to Trust You Quickly', *Fast Company*, 12 August 2015, fastcompany.com/3054275/the-secret-to-getting-other-people-to-trust-you-quickly.

Seth Godin, 'The Trap of Early Feedback', 12 February 2019, seths.blog/2019/02/the-trap-of-early-feedback.

'Locating Yourself – A Key to Conscious Leadership', The Conscious Leadership Group, 15 November 2014, youtube.com/watch?v=fLqzYDZAqCI.

Byron Katie and Stephen Mitchell, *Loving What Is: Four Questions That Can Change Your Life*, Harmony Books, 2003.

Karl Jaspers, *General Psychopathology*, Manchester University Press, 1963.

Brené Brown, *Daring Greatly: How the Courage to Be Vulnerable Transforms the Way We Live, Love, Parent, and Lead*, Penguin Books, 2012.

Colin Tipping, *Radical Self-Forgiveness: The Direct Path to True Self-Acceptance*, Sounds True, 2011.

Part II: Your triggers

Judson Brewer, 'A Simple Way to Break a Bad Habit', TED, 24 February 2016, youtube.com/watch?v=-moW9jvvMr4.

Charles Duhigg, *The Power of Habit: Why We Do What We Do in Life and Business*, William Heinemann, 2014.

Michelle Obama, *Becoming*, Penguin Books, 2018.

Stephen Karpman, *A Game Free Life*, Drama Triangle Publications, 2014.

Will Smith, 'Fault vs. Responsibility', youtube.com/watch?v= USsqkd-E9ag.

Douglas Stone and Sheila Heen, *Thanks for the Feedback: The Science and Art of Receiving Feedback Well*, Penguin Random House, 2015.

Sebastian Junger, *Tribe: On Homecoming and Belonging*, Fourth Estate, 2016.

Alessandra Edwards, *The DNA of Performance: How to Unlock Your Genes for Unstoppable Energy and Vitality*, 2020.

Sarah McKay, 'The Neuroscience of Mindfulness Meditation', The Chopra Center, 25 March 2016, chopra.com/articles/the-neuroscience-of-mindfulness-meditation.

Part III: The truth

Marcus Buckingham and Ashley Goodall, 'The Feedback Fallacy', *Harvard Business Review*, March–April 2019.

Martin E. P. Seligman, *Learned Optimism: How to Change Your Mind and Your Life*, Vintage, 2006.

Don Miguel Ruiz and Don Jose Ruiz with Janet Mills, *The Fifth Agreement: A Practical Guide to Self-Mastery*, Amber Allen, 2012.

Priya Parker, *The Art of Gathering: How we Meet and Why it Matters*, Riverhead Books, 2018.

Cy Wakeman, *No Ego: How Leaders Can Cut the Cost of Workplace Drama, End Entitlement, and Drive Big Results*, Macmillan US, 2018.

Margaret Heffernan, www.mheffernan.com.

Oriah Mountain Dreamer, *The Invitation*, HarperOne, 1999.

Don Miguel Ruiz, *The Four Agreements: A Practical Guide to Personal Freedom*, Amber-Allen Publishing, 1997.

Brené Brown, *The Gifts of Imperfection*, Hazelden Publishing, 2010.

Thomas Curran, 'Our Dangerous Obsession with Perfectionism is Getting Worse', TED, 1 April 2019, youtube.com/watch?v=lFG1b1-EsW8.

Rachel Marie Martin, *The Brave Art of Motherhood: Fight Fear, Gain Confidence, and Find Yourself Again*, Waterbrook Press, 2018.

Carol Dweck, *Mindset: The New Psychology of Success*, Random House, 2006.

Carol Dweck, 'The Power of Believing that You Can Improve', TED, youtube.com/watch?v=_X0mgOOSpLU.

Elaine Aron, 'The highly sensitive person', hsperson.com.

Jay Shetty, jayshetty.me.

Part IV: Your transformation

Eckhart Tolle, 'Concept of Enlightenment', 2008, youtube.com/watch?v=rdgO4UDrwm8.

Jeff Olson, *The Slight Edge: Turning Simple Disciplines into Massive Success and Happiness*, Momentum Media, 2005.

Steven Pressfield, *The War of Art: Break Through the Blocks and Win Your Inner Creative Battles*, Warner Books, 2002.

David Brooks, 'The Lies Our Culture Tells Us About What Matters – And a Better Way to Live', TED, 3 July 2019, youtube.com/watch?v=iB4MS1hsWXU.

Viktor Frankl, *Man's Search for Meaning*, Beacon Press, 1946.

Russell Brand, 'Vulnerability and Power (with Brené Brown)', *Under The Skin with Russell Brand*, 21 June 2019.

Brené Brown, *Rising Strong*, Spiegel & Grau, 2015.

Gabby Bernstein, gabbybernstein.com.

Cory Muscara, *Stop Missing Your Life: How to be Deeply Present in an Un-Present World*, Da Capo Lifelong Books, 2019.

Don Miguel Ruiz Jr, *The Mastery of Self: A Toltec Guide to Personal Freedom*, Hierophant Publishing, 2016.

INDEX

ABOUT GEORGIA

Georgia is not a conventional human. She's a little left of centre; a self-defined 'quirky corporate'. Her background is also atypical. She has led people and culture, marketing, sales and business development, and recruitment. She initially started as an accountant. Go figure!

The one constant in Georgia's global career has been her determination to ensure we all have real conversations – the ones we need to have with each other, including *about* each other. Her work in this space has led her to be recognised as Australia's leading expert in designing feedback cultures. She has authored two best-selling books about this: *Fixing Feedback* and *Feedback Flow*.

Georgia has worked with some of the best teams and organisations around the world including Atlassian, Telstra, Dior, Australia Post, Canva, Airtasker, The University of Melbourne, MYOB, BP and many more. She has learned that the key to any successful team is people: when they are at their best, the business is too.

Georgia is a keynote speaker, facilitator, trainer and mentor in strategic planning and workforce culture. Her MO is helping people make peace with who they are. She is a single mum to her teenagers Jacko and Holly, and lives in bayside Melbourne.

She's an avid yogi, a dinner-party lover and a self-confessed excellent reverse parker. She barely speaks French.

Visit georgiamurch.com to find out more and subscribe to Georgia's blogs to see what she is thinking about lately. You can also find her on Instagram, Facebook and LinkedIn.

NOTES

NOTES

NOTES

NOTES

NOTES

NOTES

NOTES

NOTES